ARRIVE ALIVE
the motorist's guide
to personal safety

GRAHAM YUILL A.D.I.

OTTER PUBLICATIONS
CHICHESTER, ENGLAND

First published in 1994 by **Otter Publications**, 5 Mosse Gardens, Fishbourne, Chichester, West Sussex, PO19 3PQ.

DISCLAIMER
Whilst the information herein is supplied in good faith, no responsibility is taken by either the publisher or the author for any damage, injury or loss, however caused, which may arise from the use of the information provided.

WARNING
Do not attempt any of the manoeuvres without the supervision of a Department of Transport Approved Driving Instructor who specialises in evasive and awareness driving skills.

The male pronoun has been used throughout the book. This is simply to avoid ugly and cumbersome language, and no discrimination or bias is intended.

British Library Cataloguing in Publication Data.
A Catalogue record for this book is available from the British Library.
ISBN 1 899053 00 X

Acknowledgements
Grateful thanks to Garry V. Wilson, M.A.(Hons). The illustration of a Fiat Uno (Figure 26) is reproduced with the kind permission of Fiat U.K. Limited.

Text designed by Julia Stevenson.
Cover designed by Jim Wilkie.
Chapter opening cartoons by Simon Golding.
Printed and bound in Great Britain by Hartnolls Ltd., Bodmin.
Distributed in the U.K. by Vine House Distribution, Waldenbury, North Common, Chailey, East Sussex, BN8 4DR.
The Otter Publications logo has been reproduced from original artwork by David Kitt.

Contents

Introduction

This book is aimed at <u>anyone</u> who is concerned about his own personal safety when driving behind the wheel. You may be an ordinary day-to-day citizen going about your daily business, or you may be a policeman, a security officer or serving member of the security forces, or even a well known celebrity. Whoever you are, you may one day have to use the skills covered in this book so that you can even the odds in a crisis situation.

Driving for many motorists is a necessary part of everyday life and travelling from one location to another, safely, without incident, is something which many drivers take for granted. However, driving, especially at night, can be a harrowing experience for many motorists, especially women. Many drivers feel vulnerable and are unsure about the safest course of action to take were they to be attacked. This step-by-step, easily understood book, will teach you how to keep safe, how to recognise and escape attacks, how to prevent car theft, and how to deal with other related problem situations before they become deadly emergencies.

The book is completely up-to-date; it explains all the latest devices you can buy to protect your vehicle, before moving on to show you defensive, evasive and awareness driving techniques. You will learn the J-turn, the two-point turn, the single vehicle ram, the double vehicle ram and the moving ram, etc. You will also learn how to deal with motorcycle attacks and the precautions you can take to guard against car bombs. Some of the techniques and skills covered in this book are taught and practised by members of the security forces. In addition, the book is very well illustrated with detailed aerial-view diagrams which cover every situation.

Chapter 1

The rights of a victim of attack

"You are charged with the use of excessive force, with a Woman's Own! How do you plead?"

SELF-DEFENCE

The law states that anyone who is attacked is entitled to ward off the assailant by reasonable means for his own protection. It is not always necessary for the attacker to strike the first blow if physical aggression is reasonably feared. The force must not exceed what is required to beat off the attack. However, if the attack is made with such extreme violence that the victim's life is in danger, it may be justified even to kill the assailant as a last resort. In all cases, no hard or fast rules of law apply. The court has to decide whether in all the circumstances the forces used were reasonable.

OFFENSIVE WEAPONS

In olden days, horsemen would protect themselves by riding on the left-hand side of the road, close to thick-wooded hedgerows. Since the majority of people were right-handed, they would draw their swords with their right hands in order to defend themselves if they were attacked by an enemy. With the development of modern technology, horses have now been replaced by the motor car. It is an offence to carry a sword or other offensive weapon in your car for self-defence. In fact it is illegal to carry anything in your car capable of causing injury without having a lawful reason.

USING YOUR CAR AS A WEAPON

Most people do not consider a car to be an offensive weapon. This is because it is a familiar everyday object which is taken for granted and is only perceived as being an offensive weapon when someone becomes involved in an accident. However, a motor vehicle is not a toy and in the hands of an idiot it is indeed a dangerous and lethal weapon. In the hands of a skilled driver, properly used, it can also be deadly. It is therefore essential that you know how to use your car as a weapon for self-defence if you ever feel your life is in danger.

THE MINI-MAGLITE® FLASHLIGHT

A friend of mine once struck someone on the head with a mini-maglite torch, (which was attached to his car keys), in self-defence. He was later charged with possessing an offensive weapon. However, his case did not go to court. Although the

Mini-Maglite flashlight® had been used in the attack, there was no evidence that it had originally been carried for that purpose.

The Mini-Maglite® flashlight is a very effective self-defence weapon and it can be used to restrain very violent attackers. One end has a hole drilled through it so that a key ring may be attached to it. You can use the Mini-Maglite® flashlight to poke, apply pressure or strike an opponent. Always keep your Mini-Maglite® flashlight attached to your car keys.

Chapter 2

Recognising attacks

Always remember that you can be attacked and physically assaulted at any place and at any time of the day when you are driving your car. This chapter aims to teach you how to recognise attacks before they become deadly emergencies.

DO NOT PANIC

Always remember that once an attack happens the odds are in the favour of the assailant. The secret is not to panic. Panicking is sudden and infectious fear. To avoid panicking, you must be trained to react positively with controlled aggression. When an attack does happen, you normally have split seconds to respond. If you sit and do nothing, recovering from the shock or contemplating what to do, you are at the mercy of the attacker. In a few seconds, a good driver can get himself out of any trouble.

THE SNATCH TECHNIQUE

Many attacks will take place in or near the victim's motor car. Let us look at a typical "snatch" technique used by attackers. Imagine the victim's car is travelling along the road and suddenly a vehicle pulls out of a side road which causes the victim to execute an emergency stop. The car travelling behind the victim's vehicle will then most probably crash into the rear, so adding to the crisis, or it will effectively block its rear. The assailants will then storm the victim's car, assaulting or knocking out anyone who poses a threat to them. The victim may then be forced out of the car and abducted or beaten up and perhaps dumped at the side of the road. The incident will happen very quickly and the site for the attack will be well chosen. There will be few, if any, witnesses. (See Figure 1).

There are five fatal mistakes a driver can make when an attack happens. Let us look at these five mistakes in detail.

THE FIVE FATAL MISTAKES

1. Complacency

This mistake occurs when a driver travels on the same road, carrying out the same routine day after day. This leads the driver into a false sense of security as he will be "switched off", presuming that danger will never happen. Should an attack occur, the driver's response-time will be much longer, as he must mentally work out in his head how to react in order to deal with

Victims car

Figure 1. The Snatch Technique.

the situation correctly rather than this simply being a "reflex" action.

2. Not reacting
Your attacker will not expect you to react positively if an attack happens. It could be a car-jacker or opportunist thief attempting to rob you of your possessions. It may even be a sex attacker or murderer trying to rape or kill you. By not reacting, you have played right into your assailant's hands.

3. No escape route
Imagine driving through traffic and the vehicle in front of you stops at a set of traffic lights. If you do not leave enough distance from the vehicle in front of you when you stop, another driver travelling behind you could position his car close to your rear bumper and you would be boxed in. Never get caught in between two vehicles. Anything could happen, and you will be trapped with no escape route if you are attacked. A good driver always stops his vehicle a safe distance from the vehicle in front. (See Figure 2).

4. Vehicle location
You can be at your most vulnerable if you have to reverse your car out of a driveway or from a parking space. This would give you less time to drive out of danger. It is therefore prudent to reverse into a driveway or parking space for a quick getaway.

5. Vehicle skills
Quite clearly, if a driver has not been properly trained in evasive and awareness driving skills then he will not be able to react properly should an attack happen.

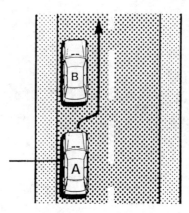

Figure 2. Always keep a safe distance from the vehicle in front.

YOU THE VICTIM

If someone has singled you out for an attack, he will most probably place you under surveillance. He will be watching your routines and may well build up a personality profile on you.

The type of details that might be included in a personality profile are as follows:

(1)   Date and place of birth.
(2)   Home and business addresses.
(3)   Family history and spouse's background.
(4)   University or college attended.
(5)   Military or police service.
(6)   Business directorships and shareholdings.
(7)   Type of employment and business contacts.
(8)   Income.
(9)   Property details.
(10) Hobbies and regular meeting places.
(11) Membership of any political party and position held.
(12) Type of vehicle(s) owned and most commonly driven.
(13) Details of close friends.

If you discover that someone is enquiring into your background in areas such as this, without your knowing of a valid reason, you should immediately be on your guard and contact the the appropriate authorities.

Chapter 3

Defensive driving

Simon

When driving, you often have to cope with unpredictable, irrational, offensive and, quite often, dangerous behaviour. To survive these conditions, it is imperative that you learn a defensive strategy. Driving instructors call this "defensive driving". This chapter aims to teach you defensive and evasive driving skills so that you can drive safely and survive on the road whilst driving.

ANTICIPATION
Since we now live in an age where violence against car drivers is on the increase, it is important to remember that you must never become complacent and you should be constantly vigilant against danger at all times when behind the wheel. This means expecting the unexpected and never being taken by surprise. You should question the actions of other road users and treat everyone as being potentially hostile until they prove otherwise. Always give yourself time and space so that you can anticipate the actions of other road users. A traffic accident may not be your fault, but fault will not be the issue for you if you are killed.

AVOIDING HOSTILITY
You should never drive in a way which provokes reaction from other drivers. For example, do not hog the right-hand lane, for someone may wish to overtake you. Although you may be driving to the maximum speed limit, other drivers may want to go faster and staying in the right-hand lane may result in open hostility, abusive language, threats, physical violence or worse! If another driver wishes to exceed the speed limit then that is his problem if he gets caught breaking the law!

THE MACHO DRIVER
The problem with many young male drivers is that they feel under pressure from their friends and their culture in general to be aggressive and macho when driving. Such ideas are reinforced by computer games which encourage young boys to overtake at great speeds and generally risk their "lives" for high scores. This behaviour is not conducive to sensible driving when they come to face life on the real roads. When they "die" playing the computer game, they lose one "life"; on the real roads, they only have one life. (See Figure 3).

Figure 3. The macho driver.

VEHICLE COMBAT

You should, at all costs, avoid getting into a situation where you may come across a driver who will try to antagonise you into "vehicle combat" or competitive driving. This type of driving creates dangerous situations; for example, the other driver may prevent you overtaking by cutting in front of your vehicle or he may slam the brakes on suddenly. Alternatively, he may try to goad you into racing against him when you are stopped at traffic lights. Such a driver often undergoes a severe personality switch, changing from a person of quite normal disposition to an irrational psychopath! If you come across such a driver, you should restrain yourself from any involvement, for obvious reasons.

PLANNED DRIVING

There will be occasions when time spent on planning your route will prevent you from getting lost and will put you in a better position to deal with any hazards which may lie ahead. When your car is in motion, always keep an eye on what other drivers are doing and be aware of the general road and traffic conditions. Make full use of peripheral vision to avoid eye contact, as this may attract attention. However, you must avoid "information overload", in other words you must not become overwhelmed with so much information that you fail to observe any real danger at all. A poorly organised visual search system will be inefficient in collecting relevant information in sufficient time for you to react safely if you are attacked. It may also cause you to over-react to an incident where there is no real danger.

HOLDING BACK

When dealing with potentially dangerous situations, there will be times when you should "go" (in other words, get your vehicle to an area of safety), times when you cannot "go" (and may have to be prepared to take defensive action) and finally, situations where you "don't know". The "go" and "don't go" situations are self-explanatory. However, if you come across actual or potential danger on the road whilst driving and you feel you do not have enough information to make the correct driving decision, then you must hold back until you receive more knowledge of the road situation so that you may make the correct decision.

KEEPING SAFE

If you are setting out on a long journey, let other people know the route you are going to take and the expected time of your arrival. Here are some other measures you can take to keep safe:

- Ensure that the car is maintained in good condition. Check the tyres, brakes and steering at the start of every journey.
- Always carry a personal alarm (obtainable from DIY shops) whilst driving and keep it where you can get access to it easily. Don't leave it at the bottom of your handbag. However, never leave your handbag on the passenger seat from where it can be snatched easily.
- Keep a map in the car, to avoid getting lost or having to ask directions, or else use an in-car or hand-held route finder. When you program your destination into the route finder it will provide you with the quickest route, it will re-route you round any traffic jam, and it will also calculate the estimated time of your arrival. This is a very useful in-car navigation aid; it enables motorists to reach their destination safely and with the minimum amount of fuss.

- Keep the rear parcel shelf free from loose objects. This will prevent any chance of injury to passengers during any enforced emergency stop.
- Ensure that the windscreen is free from smears, the windscreen wipers are in good condition and that the windscreen wash is topped up. All these measures will prevent accidents.
- Make sure that the headlights are properly adjusted. This will maximise your own vision and minimise dazzle to others.
- Never leave children alone in your vehicle. A child can easily release the handbrake or open a door.
- Always have a torch in your car.
- If you stop for petrol or for a break, take your keys with you and check the rear seat when returning to your car (someone may have climbed into the back).
- When you return to your car, study it first to see if it has been tampered with. If it has, and you sense danger, leave your car alone and inform the police immediately.
- Make sure you have your car keys ready so that you can enter your vehicle quickly. When you get into your car lock your doors immediately even when carrying a baby or holding an object.
- Remember that if your car has central locking it will unlock all the doors. Look around for any dubious-looking characters near your car before you use it.
- Avoid parking where there are hedges and walls.
- At night, always park your car in a well-lit street.
- If you have to leave your car in a tiered car park, try to position your car in a well-lit area, as near as possible to the ground floor, near a ramp and the attendant's booth or as close to the entrance as possible.
- If it is within your means, purchase a mobile phone. Some companies now do a very low-price connection and rental for the infrequent user.
- If you see an emergency or an accident, drive on and inform the police as soon as possible.
- Make sure your fuel tank is full. If you run out of fuel, change into neutral and use the momentum of the car to move to the side of the road in order top stop.
- During wintry weather conditions, check the weather forecast.

- Always carry spare fuel and make sure you are a member of a well-known motoring organisation, in case your car breaks down.
- Carry an advance warning triangle. It is simple to fold and easy to stow away.
- Carry jump leads in case you have to recharge your battery.
- In winter carry a flask containing a hot drink.
- Carry a de-icer and a window scraper.
- Never, under any circumstances, pick up a hitch-hiker – even if they appear to be in distress. This could simply be a ploy. Don't be tempted to stop, even for harmless-looking hitch-hikers. Some attackers use a good-looking girl as bait to stop drivers. As soon as the driver stops his vehicle, muggers emerge from cover and storm the vehicle.

If your car does break down and you have to walk to get help, carry out the following procedures:
- Before you leave your car, take a note of its location.
- Place your warning triangle, on a straight road, about 50 metres (55 yards), behind your car, on the road. If your car breaks down on a hilly or winding road, place the warning triangle where other drivers will see it in good time.
- Try to walk facing oncoming traffic so that no one can pull up behind you.
- If it is dark wear bright, preferably fluorescent, clothing or carry a torch so that a vehicle doesn't accidentally hit you. When there is no pavement and you have to walk on the road make sure that you keep as close to the verge as possible.
- Keep your distance from strangers (reaction space), as this will give you more time to react if you are attacked.
- Do not hitch-hike or take lifts from strangers.
- Avoid strangers by crossing the road.
- Cover up expensive-looking jewellery.
- Carry your handbag close to you in case someone grabs it.
- Keep your house keys and credit cards separate from your handbag.
- Don't take short cuts through dark alleys or across waste ground.
- If a car stops and you think someone is following you, cross the street to see if he is still tailing you. If the threat continues,

don't be embarrassed to flag down a passing motorist. If you are attacked pick up any solid object or take off your shoe so you can smash a window and then scream for help. This will surprise your attacker and may frighten him away.

- Carry your screech alarm or a powerful whistle.
- Keep change and a phone card in case you have to call a garage or friend for help.
- Avoid standing near lonely bus stops, especially after dark.
- If you are mugged and your attacker is carrying a weapon, give the robber what he wants by emptying your handbag out on the ground and run away as quickly as possible.
- If you telephone for a taxi, be careful!

PERSONAL ALARMS

A personal alarm is designed to disorientate and surprise an attacker so that you can gain valuable seconds in which to escape (the noise can also attract other people's attention). You must take advantage of the time gained so that you can run *anywhere* that is safe. Always set your alarm off immediately if you are attacked. Thrust the alarm towards your attacker's head and aim it at his or her ear. Remember a personal alarm will only confuse your attacker for a few seconds. When you have beaten off the attack inform the police immediately. The description you give to the police about the attacker may help them catch the culprit before he strikes again.

PREVENTING CAR THEFT

Some car thefts are carried out by determined professionals but the majority of cars stolen are committed by casual thieves who take advantage of an easy opportunity. A large proportion of car crimes are committed as a direct result of someone leaving a window or a door unlocked.

You can get a series of electronic sensors built into either a door, the boot or even the bonnet; they trigger an alarm if any of them are forced open.

Some cars are protected by an engine immobilisation device. The car cannot start until the driver "punches" his personal code into a key pad. To de-activate the entire security system the driver simply presses a remote control button on a key fob. A stolen car can mean having to walk home late at night. Here are some precautions you can take to prevent your car from being stolen, and some advice on how to quickly recover your vehicle if someone takes it without your consent.

- Always lock your car, even when leaving your vehicle unattended for a few seconds.
- Never leave children alone in your car. Someone may abduct your child.
- Never place items of value in your car then leave your vehicle unattended. You never know who is watching you. If it is essential to leave something of value in the vehicle, ensure it is well hidden from view.
- If your locks are worn, replace them.
- It would be a wise investment to fit a good-quality car alarm (make sure you use it at all times), or an immobiliser for extra security. A hidden cut-out switch can be cheaply fitted. You can also purchase an alarm which will activate when you press a button, either from inside or outside the car, as soon as someone attempts to steal it.
- You can get deadlocks fitted to the car doors so that they cannot be opened, even if a window has been broken.
- When you leave your car always make sure that the steering lock has been engaged and that all the windows and doors are securely shut.
- To prevent your petrol tank from being siphoned, invest in a locking petrol cap. Locking wheel nuts will prevent expensive wheels and tyres from being stolen.
- You can purchase a car radio with a security code or one which can be removed every time you park.
- You can mark the car registration number of your vehicle on your car stereo or CD player with an ultraviolet (UV) pen that will show up only under ultraviolet light. This will help the police to trace the owner if they recover your goods.
- Never leave your driving licence, MOT certificate, registration document or insurance certificate in your car. These documents can help a thief to sell your car.
- Fit the most effective handbrake, gear lever or steering-wheel clamp.
- Have your windscreen, wing mirrors, lights and windows etched with your registration number.
- Always remove the ignition key, even if your car is in your

garage. Some cars are fitted with a warning alarm to let you know if you leave your key in the ignition.

- When you park, watch out for strangers showing interest in your car; they may be planning to steal it rather than admiring it.
- Avoid parking in residential side streets or in unauthorised car parks.
- If you do not own a garage, park as close to your home as possible, preferably where you can see your car.
- If your vehicle is towing a caravan there are many security items on the market you can purchase to help you protect your caravan. Crooks have been known to drive alongside an unprotected caravan, switch the van to their vehicle (usually stolen or with false number plates) and then drive off. The theft will happen very quickly.

STOLEN VEHICLE TRACKING SYSTEM

Recent technological developments allow you to get your vehicle fitted with a small transponder unit which is hidden in your car. You *don't* have to know where it is concealed. If your vehicle is stolen, you simply inform the police and the stolen vehicle tracking system control centre. The control centre instantly sends a unique coded signal to high-powered transmitters, which activates the transponder unit hidden in your car. This unit immediately starts broadcasting a silent homing signal. Police cars equipped with special tracking computers are alerted, and the signal leads them straight to your car, almost anywhere in the UK, even if it is hidden in a garage.

If you protect your car with the stolen vehicle tracking system there is an excellent chance that if your car is stolen it will be found very quickly, thereby dramatically reducing the risk and expense of theft, increased insurance premiums and the inconvenience of having no vehicle.

THE PLUG-IN PORTABLE PHONE

Drivers can purchase a portable telephone that enables the user to summon help without leaving the car. By just plugging the power lead into the cigarette-lighter socket, services can be obtained by keying in a simple code. There is also a battery pack available for those vehicles that do not have a cigarette-lighter socket.

CAR PHONES

Do not use a mobile telephone whilst your vehicle is moving, unless in an emergency or if you are speaking into a hands-free unit. Many accidents are caused by drivers losing control of their vehicle because they are steering with only one hand on the wheel. There is another danger associated with mobile phones: under certain conditions it is possible for a mobile phone to cause a spark which could ignite petrol vapour, causing a fire or explosion, if it was being used in a petrol-filling station, for instance. Futhermore, safety researchers have discovered that hand-held phone sets could activate airbags if the car has them fitted.

DANGEROUS AREAS

Always be on your guard if you return to your vehicle (especially in a dark street) and find a flat tyre on your car. Carefully look around before changing the wheel. Someone may have slashed the tyre and be waiting to attack you when your back is turned. They could also scatter black tacks on the road to puncture your tyres when you drive off. If you feel you could be in danger changing a flat tyre, first drive to a safer area. You can purchase an aerosol inflator and sealer to repair a flat tyre. This will save you the time and effort of having to change a wheel, so you can get to safety quickly.

MULTI-STOREY CAR PARKS

Many people, especially women, have been attacked in multi-storey car parks, even during daylight hours. Indoor car parks have become havens for criminals who find them to be an ideal place in which to steal, mug, or attack their victims, rather than out on the streets. Avoid parking (especially late at night) where there is poor lighting (including on the stairs) or where the car park does not have closed-circuit television or a security firm present. Attackers can easily hide in dark corners, behind parked vehicles or support pillars, or under ramps, or stand silently in the murky shadows. After you have parked your vehicle, avoid sharing an elevator with any dubious-looking characters. It would be far safer to wait until someone else comes along whom you feel you can trust. If you see anyone acting suspiciously, or ever feel unsafe, park somewhere else. If you have to pay to leave the car park, always have some change with you so you can get out quickly.

USING AN ELEVATOR

Always look into an elevator in a multi-storey car park before you enter. Do not enter if a dubious-looking person is inside. If a suspicious-looking character enters the elevator after you, avoid eye contact and make full use of peripheral vision. Stand by the control panel and press the button for the next floor and leave the lift if you sense trouble. Never enter an elevator on your own if it is bound for the basement and you are going up. Regard basements as potential danger. If you are in a building with several floors and you are attacked, you should press as many floor buttons as possible. When the lift stops at every level you can then scream for help. You should avoid pressing the alarm button because this will stop the lift and you will be trapped in the elevator with your attacker.

USING A TAXI

You should be extremely careful if for any reason you have to abandon your car and telephone for a taxi. Many rapes by strangers reported in London involve mini-cabs. If you are phoning from a call box, don't let anyone hear you – someone could turn up later pretending to be a cab. Make sure you choose a reputable firm and ask the controller what make of car will collect you, and the driver's name. When the taxi eventually arrives, make sure the driver identifies himself and gives your name, and sit in the rear of the cab. Try and avoid unnecessary conversation (do not tell the driver any personal details about yourself) and use body language to indicate that you are not interested if you are chatted up. If you feel uncomfortable about the driver, order the taxi to stop at a busy area and get out. If you are travelling to somewhere where there is someone you know at home, it may be a sensible precaution to phone ahead so they'll expect your arrival. It is illegal for a non-hackney cab to pick up fares on the street. If a cab driver offers you a lift in this way, you should refuse and telephone for a cab from a firm you can trust. When you arrive at your destination, have your house keys ready and ask the driver to wait until you are safely inside.

JOY RIDERS

The media is full of stories of the modern-day menace on the roads: joy riders. Joy riders are usually young men high on drugs or alcohol who steal cars for kicks, destroying and dumping them later. They drive erratically and at great speed, without regard for their own safety or the safety of others. Should you come across joy riders whilst travelling on the road, you should avoid them at all costs and not confront them. You should, however, record the registration number, a description of the vehicle and occupants and the direction in which the vehicle is travelling and then inform the police as soon as possible. The police nowadays have very sophisticated means of tracking joy riders, such as helicopters armed with infra-red cameras, etc.

UNMARKED POLICE VEHICLES

If another driver indicates that he wants you to stop your vehicle at the side of the road, you should avoid doing so unless you are positively sure that it is a police officer in an unmarked police car. The signs to look for are as follows:
(1)   Blue flashing lights.
(2)   Horns blaring.
After you have stopped, ensure you are shown official identification. The police officer must also state his name, his police station and the reason he has stopped you. Often, undercover police can deliberately be dubious-looking characters, without the standard short-back-and-sides haircut, etc.

CAR-JACKING

Car-jacking is a modern term which originated in the United States of America. In some states it became an epidemic. Women are the prime targets for the highwaymen who often work in gangs and surprise their victims when they are travelling alone. Attacks usually happen when the car has stopped at traffic lights. They approach their victims from a "blindspot" and sometimes assault them before making off with their valuables. The car-jackers sometimes target specific models of cars. The thugs force their victims out of their vehicles (sometimes using extreme violence) and then steal them. The robbers have calculated that, because of recent technological developments, modern cars are so well protected by sophisticated alarms and immobilisers that it is easier to try to steal them when they are on the move. You can get an anti-hijack device fitted in your car; then if you are ever car-jacked, switch the engine off and abandon your vehicle (run away from the intruder) and permit the car-jacker to take your car. However, if the car-jacker does not key a code into the system he will be extremely disappointed when the anti-hijack device disables your vehicle shortly after he has driven away, and he may also be locked in the car.

TAILGATING

Assume you are driving along and you see a vehicle behind driving too close to your bumper. If this happens to you, simply ease off the accelerator very gradually to ensure that he overtakes. If this subterfuge fails and you feel you may be in danger, stop your car as soon as possible at a safe place (for example, a petrol station, a shop, a pub). Put your lights on and continuously sound your horn very loudly and draw as much attention to yourself as possible.

BEING FOLLOWED

If you realise you are being followed, do not increase speed, even though you may be tempted to try and get away. If you speed up, the pest who is following you will suspect that you have noticed him and that you are afraid. If you sit comfortably, hold the steering wheel firmly, drive with confidence and stay calm as this may deter him. If possible, position your car so that your pursuer cannot drive alongside you. Act assertively and do not respond to any threatening behaviour. If you know the area and expect a left turn ahead, turn without signalling at the last possible moment or when your pursuer's car is just overtaking you. If you live alone, don't drive home. He may follow you to your front door or return later to pester you.

DAZZLED BY HEADLIGHTS

If an oncoming driver dazzles you with his vehicle headlights, you should slow down and, if necessary, stop. Do not retaliate, and avoid looking directly at oncoming headlights, in case another driver dazzles you again.

MAKING PROPER USE OF MIRRORS

Many accidents are caused by drivers not making effective use

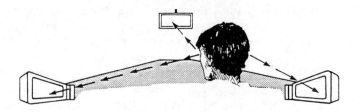

Figure 4. Making proper use of mirrors.

of their mirrors. Before you make any driving decision, the first thing you must do is check your mirrors. The mirrors are the eyes in the back of your head. Effective use of mirrors means looking and acting sensibly on what you have seen. In other words, you must Look, Assess and Decide. Do not drive with blind eyes. When you look at your mirrors, avoid staring at them, you only need to take a quick glance. If you take your eyes off the road for more than a split second, the road situation ahead could have changed and an accident may occur. (See Figure 4).

CHECK BLIND SPOTS BEFORE MOVING OFF AND BEFORE OPENING DOORS

Assume you are parked at the left-hand side of the road. Before you can drive off from a stationary position, you must always check your interior and side mirrors. However, the mirrors do not scan the whole area, therefore there is a blind spot to your off-side (right-hand side). To get round this problem you simply look over your right shoulder after you have checked your mirrors, before moving away. It is of vital importance to make these checks every time you decide to move off, in order to avoid a traffic accident. (See Figure 5).

It is permissible to quickly glance over your shoulder before you decide to change direction to the right or left, to check for other road users in the blind spot, especially motorcyclists, before joining a motorway or dual carriageway from a slip road and acceleration lane. However, if you find it necessary to check your blind spot on the move, you must be extremely careful because a vehicle in front may make a quick lane change or brake sharply when you are looking over your shoulder and not at the road in front.

Figure 5. Check blind spots before moving off and before opening doors.

GIVING PROPER SIGNALS

If you give any signal it must be given in good time, in a clear and unmistakable manner. You must signal if it would help other road users, including pedestrians. Many accidents are caused by drivers and motorcyclists signalling incorrectly and at the wrong time. Remember the routine, Mirrors, (Look Assess Decide), Signal, Manoeuvre. (See Figure 6). Making proper use of your mirrors and applying good forward observation when driving, will help you to avoid late and unnecessary signalling. Always check that your signal has been cancelled after any manoeuvre; if you fail to do this, other road users may misinterpret your intentions and an accident could occur. A word of warning: never emerge from a "give way" junction if you see another driver signalling his intention to turn. It is prudent to wait until you receive more positive information before emerging, i.e. wait until the other driver slows down and makes a definite move to turn. He may have left his indicator on by mistake.

SOUNDING YOUR HORN

You can use your horn as a signal to attract the attention of others. Always sound your horn if you have reasonable cause to do so. For example, suppose you are parked at the side of the road between two vehicles and the vehicle in front starts reversing towards you. If you believe it is not going to stop, then in these circumstances it is in fact permissible, on account of the danger, to sound the horn to warn the other driver.

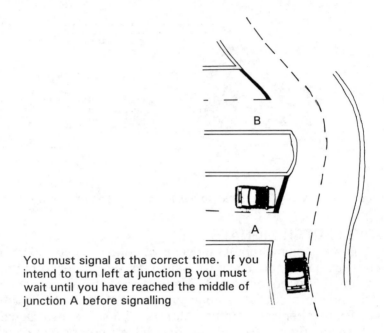

You must signal at the correct time. If you
intend to turn left at junction B you must
wait until you have reached the middle of
junction A before signalling

Figure 6. Giving proper signals.

FLASHING YOUR HEADLAMPS

Headlamps can also be used as a signal to warn other road users
of your presence; for example, during the hours of darkness,
flashing your headlamps can be a useful warning before overtaking
another driver or, during daylight hours, you may flash headlamps
in lieu of a horn warning on motorways or any other fast roads
(where, owing to the speed of the vehicles, other drivers may
not hear the horn). Flashing your headlamps means exactly the
same as sounding your horn, i.e. it lets other road users know
you are there. Do not flash headlamps at another driver or a
pedestrian for any other reason. It is dangerous, for example, to
"flash" other drivers to emerge from a side road – they must be
allowed to use their own judgement on when it is safe to do this.

CARE IN THE USE OF SPEED

Speed is far and away the most common cause of death on the

roads. A safe speed is one at which the driver can stop under full control in a safe position on the road, well within the distance known to be clear. Different types of weather conditions, the state of the road and any hazards on the road will affect the speed of your car. You should slow down and make sure you can stop safely well within the distance you can see to be clear. If you are travelling on any road outside built-up areas, it does not mean you can go as fast as you wish. You must obey the speed limits for the roads you are travelling on and the rules laid down in the Highway Code. Never accelerate into any hazard and be prepared to select a lower gear as the situation demands. A good driver always looks well ahead to avoid late and hurried driving decisions. You must always drive at a speed that is safe, even though it may be lower than what is legal. The results of a survey have shown that more than half of car drivers killed die on country roads and often no other vehicle is involved. Exercising proper care in the use of speed will get you there, even if it means arriving late. It is better to arrive late for an appointment than never to arrive at all. Imagine you are driving at 30 mph and you hit a little boy crossing the road. There is a 50/50 chance he will end up dead. If you hit him at 40 mph the chances of him surviving are virtually nil. Remember "Speed Kills"; any wally can drive fast enough to be dangerous.

MAKING PROGRESS
It can be highly dangerous not to make proper progress. Other drivers may get frustrated and take silly risks to overtake you, if you do not make normal progress to suit varying road and traffic conditions. There are two main instances of this. The first is that you are travelling too slowly for the road and traffic conditions. For example, if you are driving along a road at 20 mph, when it has a 30 mph speed limit and you could easily travel safely at 30 mph, you may inconvenience other road users for not making progress. Effort must be made by you to use the accelerator to build up the speed of your car, changing up through the gears where necessary. You must endeavour to keep up with the flow of traffic, within the speed limits. Do not reduce speed too early on the approach to a turn, as other vehicles may dart in front of you. Avoid weaving in and out between parked vehicles at short intervals. (See Figure 7).

Figure 7. Making progress.

The second way drivers often fail to make normal progress is by undue hesitancy. For example, you are sitting at a "give way" junction waiting for a gap in the traffic to appear; a gap then appears but you do not take advantage of it and instead, decide to wait. You must not be over-cautious to the point of becoming a nuisance. Try to keep your car moving at "give way" junctions if it is safe to do so. Give ways mean: give way; they do not mean: stop. Other drivers may get frustrated and take silly risks to overtake you.

OVERTAKING OTHER VEHICLES SAFELY

Most fatal traffic accidents are caused by overtaking, because it involves driving on the wrong side of the road, towards oncoming traffic. It is therefore crucial that you only overtake when it is one hundred per cent safe to do so. Never overtake unless you are sure that there is no danger to others as well as to yourself. Before you start to overtake, make sure that the road is clear far enough ahead and behind you. Remember to use the Mirrors (Look, Assess, Decide), Signal, Manoeuvre routine. On fast roads, vehicles may be coming up behind much more quickly than you imagine. Also, make sure that the lane into which you intend to move is clear far into the distance. When overtaking cyclists, always give them plenty of room, as they have a tendency to wobble, swerve or change direction without warning. Before overtaking any vehicle, you must ask yourself the following questions:

(1) Would I be breaking the law if I overtake?
(2) Can I overtake safely?
(3) Does my car have enough speed and power to overtake?
(4) Can I safely get back into my own lane in time?
(5) Do I have a safe gap to get back in?
(6) Is it necessary?

Remember the golden rule: if in doubt, DON'T.

OVERTAKING WITH DETERMINATION

Look well ahead for oncoming traffic, junctions or hazards before you decide to overtake. If it is completely safe ahead, behind and to the sides of your car you should then overtake the vehicle with determination. Remember, you are on the wrong side of the road and the less time you spend there the better. Hold a parallel course until the vehicle you have overtaken is visible in your interior mirror. By doing this, you will have moved back in well ahead of the overtaken vehicle and you will not have caused it to slow down or change direction. This will also allow space for another overtaking vehicle to pull in. There is no need to signal your intention to move back in after overtaking because other drivers would expect you to drive on the lef- hand side of the road anyway. Signalling left could make other drivers or pedestrians mistakenly believe that you intend to turn left (if there is a side road ahead) or stop on the left-hand side of the road. Signalling for the sake of signalling is a dangerous practice. Check your mirrors and increase a gear, conditions permitting.

HOLD WELL BACK

Make sure you gauge the length of the vehicle you wish to overtake. If the vehicle you are overtaking is a Heavy Goods Vehicle, you should hold well back to give yourself the best possible view past the lorry so that you can overtake once you can see that there are no hazards ahead. (See Figure 8). Be very careful, because large vehicles can often obscure hazards. If

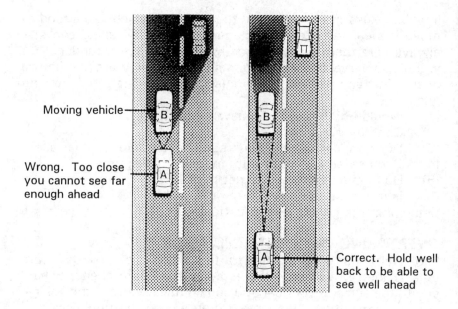

Moving vehicle

Wrong. Too close you cannot see far enough ahead

Correct. Hold well back to be able to see well ahead

Figure 8. Hold well back.

you gauge the length of the vehicle correctly, you will be able to judge how much further you will have to travel before you can safely pull back onto your side of the road. Always consider the speed of an oncoming vehicle before you decide to overtake. For example, imagine you are travelling at 50 mph and an oncoming vehicle is doing the same speed; you are approaching each other at 100 mph or 150 feet per second!

PASSING A STATIONARY VEHICLE

When approaching a parked vehicle make sure you carry out the Position, Speed, Look – Mirrors (Look, Assess, Decide), Signal, Manoeuvre routine as previously mentioned. You must Look, Assess and Decide if it is completely safe before you decide to pass any stationary vehicle. It is of the utmost importance that you check your mirrors early. You must look well ahead. If it is safe, move out from the obstruction as early as possible, leave plenty of room, and watch out for pedestrians who may step out from the other side of parked vehicles. Watch out for the parked vehicle's door opening, and keep a good safety line position. The safety line position is the safest position to adopt on the road, in relation to the actual and potential danger existing at that moment. Actual danger when passing a stationary vehicle could be a person sitting in the driving seat of his car who may decide to open his car door without looking. Potential danger could be passing a parked vehicle from behind, where a pedestrian could walk out in front of it.

ALWAYS KEEP ALERT
When you are overtaking a Heavy Goods Vehicle or a big lorry, or driving past high walls, keep both hands firmly on the steering wheel to avoid your car being "knocked" by any side draught. Take special care when you see a vehicle displaying an "L" plate or a foreign number-plate. This could indicate an inexperienced driver or one unused to driving on the left-hand side of the road.

EMERGING SAFELY AT GIVE WAY JUNCTIONS
Another area of driving fraught with danger is emerging from give way junctions. It is very important to know what you are looking for before emerging at a give way. You must look out for and give way to other vehicles, cyclists and pedestrians who may be using the road into which you are turning. Motorcycles tend to travel very fast and their riders do not always make themselves visible by wearing brightly coloured clothing. Remember as you look left, to check for any vehicles which are overtaking and are on the wrong side of the road. Do not forget that parts of your car obstruct your view so take this into consideration at all times. Watch out for any vehicles that may be emerging from a side road or driveway. They may be hidden by parked vehicles or road-side furniture. A good tip is to wind your window down, (especially in fog or at night) and listen for approaching traffic. (See Figure 9).

BE PATIENT
Never be tempted to turn or move out from a road junction because an impatient motorist has beeped his horn at you. Use your own judgement as to when it is safe. Try, however, to anticipate a safe gap in the traffic and emerge at the earliest opportunity to avoid upsetting other drivers.

Your zone of vision will completely open up when your reach point x.
Do not be foolish and emerge from the junction too soon

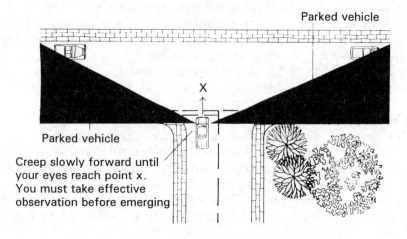

Figure 9. Emerging safely from give way junctions.

KEEP YOUR DISTANCE

Many road accidents are caused by drivers getting too close to
the vehicle in front. On the open road, in good conditions, always
keep a safe distance from the vehicle in front: a distance of one
metre for each mile per hour of your speed, or a two-second time
gap, in case the driver ahead brakes suddenly. This will also
leave space for an overtaking vehicle to pull in. On wet or icy
roads, the gap should, at least, be doubled. In any case, this is
a sensible precaution to prevent road accidents. Drop back if an
overtaking vehicle pulls into the gap in front of you. If you do not
leave enough distance from the vehicle in front, you will make it
easier for the other driver to force you to stop, and if you are
rammed from behind you will have no escape route. (See Figure
10).

THE MEAT IN THE SANDWICH

When you are driving on a narrow road, you may come across a
situation where you will meet other vehicles. This situation usually
arises when driving in a built-up area and ahead of you, you can
see there are two parked vehicles, one at the left-hand side of

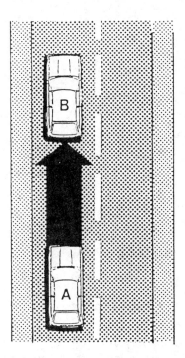

Figure 10. Keep your distance.

the road and the other at the right-hand side, possibly directly opposite each other. This can be termed a "bottleneck". A problem arises when you see another vehicle approaching and, because of timing, it is obvious that both vehicles are going to reach the bottleneck at the same time. The one thing you must not do is speed up and try to get through the gap before the other driver. This is very dangerous because the other driver might do the same and this often results in an emergency stop being carried out at the last moment or something worse. There's an old saying, "Never be the meat in the sandwich". Never be the idiot to get caught in between two vehicles, anything could happen and you will be trapped with no place to go. A good driver always looks well ahead and scans the area for any possible signs of danger and acts as the situation demands. (See Figure 11).

Figure 11.   The meat in the sandwich.

DEALING WITH TRAFFIC LIGHTS

Far too many road accidents are caused by drivers ignoring a red light and wrongly crossing your path. It is important that you observe traffic lights early and treat them with caution. Don't forget to regulate your speed correctly on the approach, and always take effective observation before emerging, in case you have to stop. Furthermore, if the traffic lights fail, proceed with extreme caution.

DEALING WITH CROSSROADS

It is important to remember that all crossroads are dangerous and they must be treated with caution. Although you may have priority, there is nothing to stop a vehicle or cyclist pulling straight out in front of you. You must always take effective observation before emerging. Moreover, there is one particular type of crossroad that is often an accident blackspot; it is the unmarked crossroad. This is potentially the most dangerous type of junction. Some drivers just drive straight through without slowing down, thinking they have priority.

DEALING WITH LEVEL CROSSINGS

Many drivers and their passengers have been killed at railway level crossings. Always approach and drive over a level crossing with vigilance and caution. A driver should **never** enter a crossing until the road is clear. It is of paramount importance to avoid driving too close to another vehicle over the level crossing.

It is also important that the driver should **never** stop on or just after the crossing, or park near the level crossing.

If your vehicle breaks down, or if you have an accident on a railway crossing, you **must** carry out the following procedure immediately to remain safe.

- Get everyone out of your vehicle and tell them to stand a safe distance from the crossing.
- Look out for a railway telephone and use it immediately to tell the signal operator your predicament.
- Follow the instructions given by the signalman.
- If it is practical (providing there is time), before a train arrives, move your vehicle clear of the crossing.
- If you hear an alarm or see an amber light, abandon your vehicle and move quickly away from the crossing.

DEALING WITH ROUNDABOUTS

When you approach a roundabout look well ahead for the advance warning signs. These signs will depict the layout of the roundabout, show route directions, and give you advance warning of the appropriate traffic lanes at the roundabout. You should select in good time the most appropriate lane in which to approach the roundabout. Do not straddle or change lanes at the last moment.

Gently reduce the speed of your car. Start looking early to your right, in order to monitor the amount of traffic already on the roundabout, as well as other vehicles emerging into the roundabout. If it is not safe to proceed at the roundabout, you must stop and give way. Remember a give way sign means give way. You do not have to stop, only stop if it is necessary. If you stop needlessly, you may hold up other traffic, causing inconvenience or even an accident. When you are looking to the right at a roundabout it is important that you use peripheral vision so that you can keep an eye on the vehicle in front, in case it stops without warning. Many accidents occur this way. You must always look forward and check that the vehicle in front has definitely moved away before you enter the roundabout.

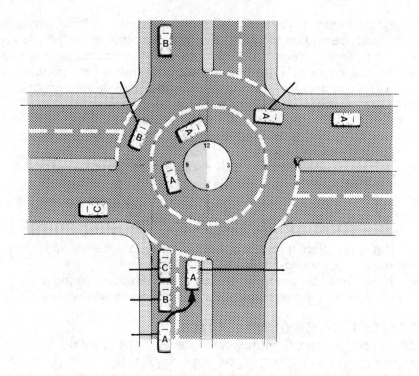

Figure 12. Dealing with roundabouts.

Remember, larger vehicles (especially Heavy Goods Vehicles drawing trailers), require more berth. They may have to manoeuvre into an unusual position whilst negotiating a roundabout.

A word of warning: a driver's zone of vision on the approach to a roundabout can be obstructed by road-side furniture, so be careful. You must always STOP and give way to traffic from the immediate right, if you are in any doubt. Finally, don't assume when driving on a roundabout that you will continue to have priority, you may occasionally see traffic lights, road signs or markings telling you that you have to give way to other traffic. So be careful. (See Figure 12).

AVOID ACCIDENTS WHILST MANOEUVRING
Before reversing carry out all-round observations and give way to other road users because you will be travelling in the wrong

direction. Turn well round in your seat and look out the rear window. Reverse very slowly, particularly if people are standing nearby. Always remember before you reverse, it must be safe, legal and convenient. You may release your seat belt for ease of movement. A very important point to remember when reversing is that you should always think which way your front wheels are pointing.

EMERGENCY VEHICLES

If you see blue flashing lights or hear the siren of a police, fire brigade, ambulance or any other emergency vehicle, you must take whatever action is possible, with safety, to allow that vehicle clear passage. However, if you come across the incident the emergency vehicle is attending, you must concentrate on what is happening ahead or you could cause another accident.

DEALING WITH A TRAFFIC ACCIDENT

Many people panic or freeze when they are involved in a traffic accident. If you are involved in a traffic accident, always keep calm and carry out the following procedures:

(1) **Stop** at the scene, if any person has been injured or if there is damage to any other vehicle, property or licensed animals.

(2) Switch your engine off; ask other drivers involved to do the same.

(3) Extinguish any cigarettes – there may be petrol leakage.

(4) Tell your passengers to leave your vehicle and get them to a place of safety. If any of your passengers are seriously injured, it would be wise to leave them in the vehicle and administer first aid.

(5) Warn other traffic.

(6) Call the ambulance service and the police.

(7) At night make sure no one stands at the rear of your vehicle, they may obscure the lights.

(8) Try and move any vehicle if it is causing danger to other traffic, ask an independent person to note the original positions of vehicles.

You can purchase a special hammer with a chromium-plated head and a razor-sharp blade so that you can shatter the side window of your car and cut the seat belt if you are trapped during a crash. The hammer comes with a plastic holder which is easily attached inside the car. It also has a fluorescent knob so you can locate it more easily in the dark.

SURVIVING IN FOG

Fog is one of the most dangerous weather conditions in which to drive. Some horrific accidents occur during fog. In thick fog, some lunatics drive at very high speeds, even though their visibility is seriously reduced. These crazy drivers cause pile-ups which sometimes involve dozens of vehicles. You must be extremely careful when you are driving in these conditions if you want to stay alive. Driving in fog can cause eye strain and your ability to anticipate the actions of other road users will be severely restricted.

When driving in fog:

- Check your mirrors and slow down. Keep a safe distance. You should always be able to pull up within your range of vision.
- Don't hang on to someone else's tail lights – it gives a false sense of security.
- Watch your speed; you may be going faster than you think. Do not speed up to get away from a vehicle which is too close behind you.
- Obey any warning signals. They are there to help and protect you.
- See and be seen. Use dipped headlights or front fog lamps. Only use rear fog lamps when visibility is severely reduced. Use your windscreen wipers and de-mister.
- Check and clean your windscreen, lights, reflectors and windows whenever you can.
- Remember that fog can drift rapidly and is often patchy. Even if it seems to be clearing, you can suddenly find yourself back in thick fog.
- Drive in the left-hand lane of motorways and dual carriageways as much as possible.
- Open your window(s) so that you can hear any approaching traffic and keep your foot on the brake pedal (an extra warning for drivers behind) if you are waiting to turn at a road junction. Consider using your horn to warn other road users of your presence.

DRINKING AND DRIVING

In a survey carried out in the United Kingdom, one in five deaths on the road were caused by drivers who had been drinking. Many drivers mistakenly believe that they are safe to drive because they have only consumed a very small amount of alcohol. In fact, even the smallest amount of alcohol can increase a driver's reaction time and cause him to misjudge distance and the speed of oncoming vehicles. Various circumstances can account for the variation in time it takes to metabolise alcohol. Some people have more effective livers than others, but the combination of height, weight and body water content is an acknowledged factor. It has been medically proved that alcohol is quickly absorbed

Figure 13. Do not put pedestrians under pressure to cross the road.

into the bloodstream, which affects the brain and impairs driving ability. Drivers also have a greater tendency to take risks, particularly in dangerous manoeuvres such as overtaking. Drinking and driving is irresponsible and extremely dangerous. Remember, someone may be driving with their alcohol level at nearly zero and driving perfectly legally, but their performance is still less than it would be if they had not been drinking at all. The only way to stay alive is *not* to drink and drive.

DRUNKEN PEDESTRIANS

We are all aware of the dangers and consequences of drinking and driving. However, another menace on the road is the drunken pedestrian. In a survey of traffic accidents involving pedestrians, in the United Kingdom, a quarter of these pedestrians were found to be under the influence of alcohol. They wander or stagger off the pavement onto the road, into the path of vehicles, causing them to swerve. Swerving suddenly to avoid a pedestrian can be highly dangerous, as you may hit or be struck by another vehicle overtaking you, or you may even collide with oncoming traffic. You should therefore apply good forward planning whilst driving and be particularly mindful of drunken pedestrians who may step out from behind parked vehicles without warning. When you are approaching parked vehicles, always look underneath them so you can see if there are feet moving beyond them. Watch the behaviour of drunken pedestrians at all times so that you can anticipate their actions and stop safely. Take extra care at night, especially when passing places where people socialise and drink.

HOW TO AVOID ACCIDENTS WITH PEDESTRIANS

Take account of pedestrians and animals, and be prepared to slow down or perhaps stop if they run out in front of you without any warning. Elderly people, who are less alert, need more time to cross the road; give them plenty of time. Never put them under pressure to cross the road quickly or leave them stranded in the middle of the road. Children are unpredictable, and they rely on you for their safety. Many children die in road accidents every year. The vast majority of these happen in built-up areas where the speed limit is 40 mph or less. Look out for people with white walking sticks or guide dogs. Remember that some people who are deaf or hard of hearing will not hear your car approaching. (See Figure 13).

Figure 14. Give way to pedestrians.

Before turning a corner you must ensure that you "look" early as you approach the corner. If you start looking in good time you will be able to see any potential dangers in the road into which you are turning. Be especially mindful of pedestrians and give way to anyone who is ready to step off the pavement or has already stepped onto the road. Your vision may be restricted into your new road, and there will be a strong possibility that you may conflict with other traffic. Remember that, in addition, your vision may be obstructed by tall hedges, buildings, or parked vehicles. Before you turn, look in the direction that you intend your car to go, and make the turn neat, clean and sharp. As your car straightens up, it should stay parallel to the kerb. Do not swing inwards to the kerb or outwards to the centre of the road. (See Figure 14).

You must always remember, that once you have decided to turn into the corner, the speed of your car must be completely under control, and you must maintain the same speed throughout the corner. Accelerating into a corner too quickly is a dangerous practice. If your speed is not under complete control, you may cause your car to skid, or you may drive "blind" into some danger, without having time to brake.

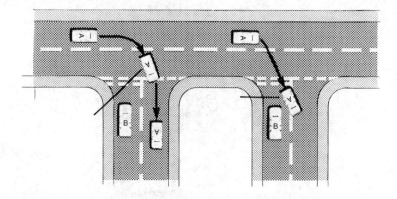

Figure 15. Cutting right-hand corners.

As soon as you are safely round the corner, cancel your indicator, (if necessary), check your mirrors and apply the accelerator, (conditions permitting), then select a good safety line position parallel with the new road. Remember, you must never accelerate if another vehicle is overtaking you.

CUTTING RIGHT-HAND CORNERS
Avoid cutting the right-hand corner. This is a dangerous practice because it will put you on the wrong side of the road. (See Figure 15). Before you turn, make a final right-hand mirror check, in case somebody is foolish enough to overtake you on the right-hand side. Always look into the road you wish to turn into for any possible danger. Remember to look and assess the situation before you decide whether it is safe to make any driving decision.

ANIMALS IN THE STREET
If you are driving at speed, do not brake or swerve to avoid a dog or cat darting out in front of you if other vehicles are travelling closely behind you. The driver behind could run into your rear or you may even collide with oncoming traffic. It may seem cruel, but it is far safer to hit the animal, even though this is the last thing you want to do. Many people have been seriously injured or killed when drivers have swerved suddenly to avoid a dog or cat.

DRIVING ABROAD

More and more people drive abroad nowadays, but this can be unsafe if you are not properly prepared. It would be prudent to contact any of the major motoring organisations so that you can plan your trip with safety and peace of mind. The major motoring organisations provide invaluable information and advice on computerised routes, motoring regulations, correct documentation and emergency telephone numbers. They can also provide cover for roadside assistance or emergency garage repairs; vehicle recovery or collection; car hire, fares and hotel accommodation: legal protection; and emergency credit for motoring abroad. It is also important to remember that in some Islamic countries there are different laws regarding women driving. You can be at your most vulnerable to muggers when you are driving in known tourist areas. Attacks usually happen when driving a rented car because the attackers can then easily identify you as a tourist. If you are hiring a car at your vacation destination, avoid collecting it at night but instead hire a taxi to your hotel or apartment. When you collect the car the following morning plan the safest route back and take time to familiarise yourself with the location and function of the car's minor and auxiliary controls before leaving the rental company's premises. Moreover, try not to dress like a tourist. Hide your wallet or purse in concealed, zipped or button pockets. Try not to dress conspicuously – that means no Hawaiian shirts, shorts or sandals, especially when it is raining.

The Channel Tunnel

The Channel Tunnel is one of the most remarkable feats of engineering ever undertaken. Journey time between platforms is 35 minutes, 27 minutes being underground, loading and unloading time taking 8 minutes. At peak times there is a 24 hour service every 15 minutes. However, there is fear and trepidation in the minds of many drivers regarding the safety of the tunnel – thankfully, these doubts are unfounded.

The tunnel is buried 150 feet beneath the seabed for most of its route and is bored through a thick, watertight layer of chalk. Drivers sit in their cars, although you may leave your car if you wish. An aerial built along the train allows people to listen to their car radio. The ventilation system has been designed to extract car fumes rapidly.

In the event of fire, foam-injection systems and fire

extinguishers are activated. Even if these fail, passengers are able to pass through a fire barrier to another carriage. The carriages are designed to withstand the worst blaze for at least 30 minutes allowing the train to reach one of the terminals. Each carriage has two emergency doors wide enough for wheel-chairs. If the fire was so bad that the train could not be moved, passengers are able to walk safely through cross-passages leading into the service tunnel.

Security measures include the routine use of electronic devices capable of detecting plastic and other types of military explosives, and x-ray machines located at each terminal will screen vehicles. Even the potential hooligan has been considered. The guard has full video surveillance and each carriage has an alarm button.

MOTORWAY DRIVING

Every year thousands of people are killed or maimed in road accidents. Some horrendous accidents occur on motorways. On motorways, you will be driving at very high speeds, especially if driving abroad. High-speed motoring is safe if it is carried out with skill and responsibility.

Before driving on the motorway

Before you decide to drive on the motorway, it is imperative that you check the general condition of your car, because you will probably be driving at high speeds. You should always check that your tyres are in good condition and the tread depth is within the legal limit. It is important that your tyre pressures are set correctly. Make sure you have enough fuel and oil, and also check the water levels. Ensure your windows, headlights, indicators and mirrors are clean. If you are drawing a trailer, check and secure the load before commencing your journey. If you feel tired or unwell do not under any circumstances drive on the motorway. You may fall asleep and possibly kill yourself or someone else.

Feeling tired

If you ever feel tired whilst driving on the motorway, wind your window down for ventilation and leave the motorway at the next exit or the nearest service station. In a detailed survey carried out in the United Kingdom and the USA, researchers found that many motorway accidents were caused by drivers falling asleep at the wheel. Most accidents happened between 4 a.m. and 6 a.m. The investigators also found that sleep-related accidents were three times more likely to result in serious injury or death than any other road accident. This was because sleepy drivers failed to brake to try to prevent the accident – so the impact was worse. Their study also revealed that many drivers found long-distance motorway driving very monotonous. This caused them to daydream whilst driving, often going into "trances". In fact, the survey also revealed that many long-distance drivers had absolutely no recollection of large parts of their journey. Remember, "Stay Awake, Stay Alive".

Using the hard shoulder

If something falls off your car when driving on the motorway, move over to the hard shoulder as soon as it is safe. Many pedestrians are killed or seriously injured whilst standing or walking on the hard shoulder. Try to position your car as far over to the left-hand side of the hard shoulder as possible. Warn any passengers of the dangers of passing vehicles and place a warning triangle approximately 150 metres to the rear of your car. This will help to prevent you from being struck by another vehicle which may be positioned badly in the left-hand lane. Look out for a telephone symbol with an arrow to tell you where the nearest emergency telephone is. (These telephones are directly connected to a police control room). Do not under any circumstances cross the central reservation to use an emergency telephone.

When rejoining the left-hand lane, build up your speed first on the hard shoulder. Wait for a safe gap in the traffic before emerging. Watch out for any motorway speed restrictions or flashing light signals which will warn you of any hazards ahead. You will usually see them on overhead gantries or at the side of the carriageway. If you ever see any flashing amber lights, check your mirrors and if it is safe, use progressive braking to slow down (especially in poor weather conditions) until you are satisfied that it is safe to go faster again.

THE KILLER OVERTAKE

Many serious and fatal accidents are caused by the killer overtake. Some drivers perform the killer overtake unintentionally – whilst attackers can use it intentionally. This scenario occurs when the driver in front moves out to overtake another vehicle and you follow behind him (even after first checking the road ahead is

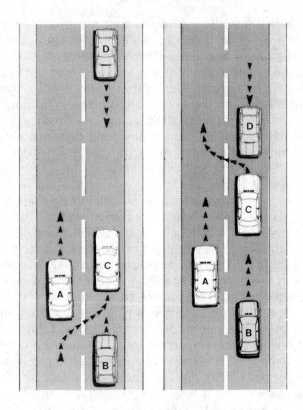

Fig. 16. The killer overtake.

clear far into the distance). When he is just past the vehicle he
is overtaking, he then waits in the same position level with this
vehicle on the inside until another vehicle appears in the distance
heading directly towards him. The driver will then accelerate
past the vehicle he is overtaking and move quickly into the inside
lane. You will then be left to collide with the oncoming vehicle.
(See Figure 16).

THE GOLDEN RULE
You must be aware of the acceleration capability of your car so
that you can move out of the "danger period" as soon as possible.
Overtaking could be the last decision you will ever make if it is
the wrong one. Remember the golden rule: if in doubt, DON'T.

Chapter 4

Attack counter-measures

Driving on your own, especially at night, can be a heart-pounding experience for many motorists, especially women. Many drivers feel vulnerable and unsure about the safest course of action to take if they are approached or attacked. This chapter deals with the precautions you can take to safeguard your vehicle and how to defend yourself if you are being attacked when driving your car.

TYPES OF ATTACKERS

Before we begin to look in detail at how you should keep safe behind the wheel of your car, you must understand that there are always men and women who are prepared to use violence to achieve their aim. Violence is a phenomenon which people naturally fear, for hardly a day passes without news of fatal assaults. The men and women who use violence, for whatever motive, can be classified into the following groups:

- Opportunist (someone who does not plan an attack but may react to an "easy target").
- Psychopath (mentally impaired individual, unable to stop killing).
- Someone affected by drink or drugs (they have some effect on the brain and change the user's emotions or mental state).
- Robber (someone who plunders or steals from another).
- Sex attacker (most commonly strike at night).
- Fanatic (someone who acts for a cause they are obsessive about, often a terrorist).

DEALING WITH CAR-JACKERS

When you are driving in a busy area, it is highly probable that you will come across a set of traffic lights. Car-jackers often operate at traffic lights as the driver may have to stop and give way to pedestrians if the traffic lights are red. When driving, always scan the road ahead and to the side, looking for any potential dangers. As you approach a set of traffic lights, you should be ready to accelerate out of danger should anyone attempt to force you to stop. If you have to stop at a set of traffic lights, watch out for anyone approaching your car (he may come from a "blind spot"). You are most at risk from car-jackers if you dress ostentatiously. Remember, "if you've got it, be careful where you flaunt it". If someone approaches your car with the intention

of speaking to you, carry out the following procedures:
- Make sure all your doors are locked.
- Keep your valuables out of sight.
- Under no circumstances unlock any of your doors.
- Pretend you are using your car telephone (authentic-looking dummy car telephones are also available).
- Lower your window only about 10 cm if he wants to speak to you. If you wind your window down too far he may grab you or punch you in the face.
- Do not switch your ignition off (you may have to drive off out of danger).
- If it is someone, in plain clothes or in uniform claiming to be a police officer, ensure identification is produced and that you examine it.

Should he appear to be threatening you, consider "jumping" the traffic lights but only if it is safe for you to do so.

If for any reason it is not possible for you to "jump" the traffic lights, carry out the following procedures:
- Keep calm and do not panic.
- Move to the centre of your car.
- Consider using your horn – or activate your panic alarm, in case the intruder smashes a window and opens any of the doors.

Use the following equipment that you may have in your car to defend yourself, if necessary:

(1)	De-icer (you may have to shake the contents first).
(2)	Torch.
(3)	Hair/anti-perspirant spray.
(4)	Pen or pencil.
(5)	Fire extinguisher.
(6)	Rolled up newspaper or magazine.
(7)	Mini-Maglite® flashlight.
(8)	Scissors, metal nail file or comb.

Keep them all within easy reach. If you are attacked and you feel your life is in danger, try to aim at his eyes for maximum effect. Consider striking your attacker with your car door. Always use controlled aggression with speed. Should any of those techniques fail, you can carry out any of the following self-defence techniques.

Hair or ear grab

Grasp your attacker's hair. With enough aggression you can pull him all over the place and simultaneously strike him on the head with your Mini-Maglite® flashlight. If your attacker has short hair grab his ear.

Eye poke

It is impossible for anyone to build up the muscles in their eyes. To cause serious injury, poke him in the eyes with two fingers. Then follow up with another strike to the head with your Mini-Maglite® flashlight.

Throat grab

This is the most effective attack. Grasp the assailant's throat firmly and then quickly strike him with your Mini-Maglite® flashlight. You could also do a "karate chop" to the throat.

BEING CAPTURED

If someone succeeds in entering your vehicle and forces you to drive to an area, you must know how to handle this frightening situation before you reach your assailant's planned destination, by which time it may be too late for you to react. Your attacker may threaten you with an offensive weapon or he may even grab your hair, shouting and threatening you with violence if you fail to comply with his instructions. Do exactly as your assailant tells you. However, if you feel your life is in danger, you should gradually build up the speed of your car until you reach a very fast speed. As soon as this happens, tighten your grip on the steering wheel, then slam on the footbrake as hard as possible (providing your attacker has not fastened his seat belt). If you brake hard enough, your assailant will be projected forward very quickly and he will most probably be thrown through the windscreen, or he may rebound back and forward off it, almost certainly knocking him unconscious or severely injuring him. You may have to endure some pain if your attacker has a good firm grip on your hair when he is being projected forward, although the shock of what is happening will probably make him release his grip. If your assailant has fastened his seat belt during the attack, don't worry, but surreptitiously release his seat belt just before you brake very hard. His anchor point will be situated near your seat. Just make sure you choose his release button – and not your own! After the attacker has been thrown from the car, you should speed away as quickly as possible. If your attacker is still inside your car, you should use your judgement as to whether it is better to push him from your vehicle or leave the vehicle and run. If the attacker is armed with an offensive weapon, it is probably best to get away from him immediately in case he lashes out at you; you should push him out only if you are sure he is definitely totally unconscious. If the area where you have stopped is populated, it will also be safer to leave the car and run towards help. If you feel you have to leave the car in an unpopulated area, try to grab the car keys before escaping or choose a route where a car could not pursue, over fences or across fields, for example.

You or him
Always adopt a mental attitude of no mercy: a rapist or killer will show you none.

DRIVING AT NIGHT
If you are driving along a dark country road and you are forced by an attacker to stop your vehicle, you should carry out the following procedures:
(1)   Immediately put on main beam and your spot lights.
(2)   Activate your car alarm. This may cause the attacker to panic or it may attract attention if there is anyone in the vicinity.
(3)   Grab your torch.
(4)   Abandon your car.
(5)   Move quickly into the shadows.
If you act very quickly, this can be a very effective technique, as your strong lights will momentarily blind your attacker which will give you enough time to escape.

USING A TORCH
It is a proven fact that using a strong light and loud noise simultaneously can disorientate an assailant. You can purchase several torches that have a very powerful beam and sirens capable of causing an attacker to panic and become disorientated when they are activated.

Attackers may also attempt to make use of torches. They may approach your car from behind, pointing the torch into your wing mirror so you cannot watch what he is doing without being dazzled or he may appear at your side window, pointing the torch at your face, attempting to disorientate you. The important thing is to avoid looking directly at the beam and follow the other guidelines given in this book.

ATTACK COUNTER-MEASURES

Here are some counter-measures that you can implement to avoid being attacked whilst driving:

- Try and travel with more than one person in the car.
- Close surveillance should be kept on accompanying traffic from the front and rear.
- Be particularly mindful of vehicles and motorbikes which draw up alongside you at traffic lights.
- Avoid opening your window more than 10 cm to prevent someone throwing a missile through the window.
- Beware of overtaking vehicles, especially on remote roads.
- Drive on major roads if possible.
- Consider using your car as a weapon if you are attacked.
- Always lock your doors to avoid unauthorised entry.
- Avoid routines. Vary your routes.
- Keep alert and be observant at all times.
- If you stop your vehicle in a situation where you feel unsure, do not turn off your engine as it may not start again.
- If another motorist attempts to make you stop by flashing his lights and indicating a fault on your car, acknowledge their signal, do not stop but drive to where you feel safe.

BEING RAMMED FROM BEHIND

If another driver crashes into the rear of your vehicle, you should use your judgement as to whether it is better to leave the safety of your car and exchange particulars with the other driver, to signal the driver to follow you and proceed to a safe, well-lit area, or to drive *immediately* to the nearest police station (try and record the other vehicle's registration number) and report the accident. You should *only* drive to the police station if you feel you may be in danger. The police will be very sympathetic to you and will approve the course of action you have taken, especially if you are a lone woman driver.

Some attackers use a stolen car so that they can ram the rear of another vehicle. As soon as the victim leaves the car the assailants will then attack the driver or anyone who poses a threat to them.

IF YOU HAVE BEEN ATTACKED

If someone seriously assaults or rapes you, contact the police as soon as possible. Do not wash or bathe yourself until you have been examined by a doctor. Washing can destroy forensic evidence.

Chapter 5

Dealing with emergencies

BREAKING DOWN ON THE MOTORWAY

If your car breaks down whilst travelling on the motorway, move over to the hard shoulder at the earliest and safest opportunity. Try to cruise your car as far over to the verge as possible in case you have occasion to repair a puncture on the driver's side of the car. Remember, the hard shoulder is a very dangerous place to stop. Don't open any of the doors on the driver's side. Make sure you and all your passengers leave the vehicle from the passenger side and stand on the embankment away from the hard shoulder. Also try to place your car as near as possible to an emergency telephone. Switch on your hazard lights to warn other drivers you have broken down. Position your warning triangle about 150 metres (165 yards) back from the car to warn other drivers. Roadside markers may guide you to the whereabouts of the nearest emergency telephone. If someone approaches you whilst you are using the telephone (even if they appear genuine) give a description to the police at the control centre of what the person looks like and then take the registration number if he is driving a motor vehicle. Inform the stranger that you gave the police all his details. If he has criminal intent this will frighten him away. It has been known for motorists to be attacked and killed even in broad daylight near the hard shoulder.

If for any reason it is not possible for you to reach an emergency telephone, you have the following options to chose from:

Option 1

Stay in your car, making sure it is as far away as possible from the carriageway. By doing this you will be less likely to be struck by other vehicles. Lock all doors, to prevent unauthorised entry, and sit in the front passenger seat with your seat belt on in case your car is shunted from the rear. By sitting in the passenger seat you can give the impression that you are waiting for the driver to come back. It would be prudent to keep the lights on to enable other drivers to see you. The police or a major motoring association will eventually notice your predicament and come to your assistance, although you may have to wait for some time. It is highly advisable that you should join a major motoring association because they provide numerous services and usually arrive within the hour. The longer you have to wait at the side of the carriageway, the greater the danger you may be in. Many breakdowns attended by motoring associations could easily be prevented if your car is regularly serviced at a reputable garage or if you have knowledge of basic car maintenance.

Option 2
You may feel safer leaving your car and climbing over the barrier or up the bank at the side of the motorway. You can wait near your car but out of sight of passing motorists. Do not attempt to repair your car or cross to the other side of the motorway to use an emergency telephone – many accidents occur when vehicles hit stationary cars on the hard shoulder. Leave the passenger door open and be ready to leap back in and lock the door behind you if another driver stops who, you feel, looks suspicious. It is a good idea to pack waterproof or extra warm clothing, spare boots and blankets before setting out on a long journey. You can use this spare clothing to keep you warm and dry should you have to wait for a long period of time. Stranded drivers (especially the disabled) should display a help pennant. A passing motorist may then alert the police or the emergency services.

A person claiming to be from the emergency services should produce to you:
(1)   Proof of identification.
(2)   Your name.
(3)   The information you revealed to the control centre about the breakdown.

Remember, judge each circumstance on its merit; there is no golden rule for all situations.

ACCEPTING A LIFT
You should always avoid accepting a lift from a stranger, but if, for some pressing reason, this is unavoidable, it is a good idea to make sure you fail to shut the door properly so that you have to open it again. This will enable you to see how the door opens and whether there is a lock which has to be released first. If you smoke, light up a cigarette and be prepared to stab it in the driver's face (try and aim it at his eyes) if he attacks you. If you feel you may be in danger, leave the car quickly if it stops at traffic lights. You could also pretend you are feeling ill and that you are going to be sick. Put on an act and start burping then

ask him to stop at the side of the road so that you can escape. If this subterfuge fails, you should consider more dramatic actions such as jerking the handbrake on or grabbing the steering wheel (in a road where it is reasonably safe to do so).

STOPPING IN AN EMERGENCY

If you have to stop your vehicle in an emergency, the amount of pressure you apply on the footbrake will depend on the road conditions. If the road is good, firm and dry, you can push the brake pedal harder as the car slows down. However, if the road surface is wet and loose, you will have to brake less firmly. If the brake is applied too hard, you may skid. Moreover, your brakes can be your worst enemy on wet or icy roads. If you can't stop in time it may be better to steer carefully round something than to slide into it. Remember if your brakes and tyres are not in first- class condition you will take longer to stop.

THE MAIN CAUSES OF SKIDDING

There are three different types of skids that may occur if you are driving a motor car. They are a front-wheel skid, a rear-wheel skid and a four-wheel skid. There are four main causes of skidding: excessive speed, harsh braking, fierce acceleration and erratic steering. A good driver never gets caught in a skid. If you are looking well ahead and driving at a speed appropriate to the road and traffic conditions, a skid will never happen.

THE CORRECTION OF SKIDS

In case your car gets involved in a skid, you must know what caused the skid and the most effective way to correct it. As soon as you apply harsh pressure to the footbrake the occupants and the full weight of your car are thrown forwards, making the rear of your car much lighter. As soon as this happens the rear wheels could lose their grip on the road. If you apply too much pressure on the acceletaor the occupants of your car are pressed back in their seats, making the weight of your car much lighter at the front, and the front wheels could lose their grip on the road. If your car is cornering too fast, the occupants of your car are thrown sideways, and a skid could again occur.

The rear-wheel skid

If your rear wheels lose their grip on the road and the rear of your

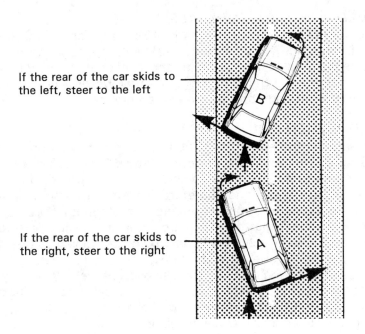

If the rear of the car skids to the left, steer to the left

If the rear of the car skids to the right, steer to the right

Figure 17. The rear-wheel skid.

car swings either to the right or the left, you are in a rear-wheel skid. As soon as you realise this is happening, you must take your foot off the brake pedal and turn the steering wheel in the direction of the skid. If the rear wheels slide to the left, turn the steering wheel to the left. You can re-apply the footbrake as soon as you have regained control. (See Figure 17).

The four-wheel skid

If you feel your car sliding helplessly out of control in any direction, you are in a four-wheel skid. To correct this, simply relax the pressure on the footbrake. This will allow the wheels to re-grip the road again and then pump the footbrake on and off (not too quickly) until your car regains control. Make sure you apply maximum pressure to the footbrake and release it just as the wheels are about to lock before re-applying pressure again. This is an excellent technique to use if the road conditions are very slippery.

Anti-locking braking systems (ABS)
If your car is fitted with anti-lock brakes, they can be extremely useful in an emergency. When the wheels are about to lock, a sensor control releases the brake and applies it again, which is really automatic rhythmic braking. In other words, you can keep the pressure on and steer at the same time.

DEALING WITH FIRE
Many serious and sometimes fatal accidents can be prevented by taking correct and prompt action should fire break out in the engine compartment of your vehicle. Fire can spread through a vehicle in seconds. It is therefore essential that you always carry a fire extinguisher in your vehicle at all times. If you smell burning or suspect that there is a fire in the engine compartment, you must stop your vehicle at a safe place as quickly as possible and switch the engine off. The first priority is for the safety of any passengers who may be travelling in the vehicle with you. Make sure they all exit as quickly as possible by selecting the safest route and keep them well away from the car. Contact the fire brigade immediately. Under no circumstances open the bonnet wide as you will create a draught of air which will fan the fire and you may cause a mini-fireball. Many drivers have been seriously burned in this way. As soon as you open the bonnet slightly, direct your fire extinguisher through the small gap and fully extinguish the fire. If you do not have a fire extinguisher in the car, you should avoid opening the bonnet and call the fire brigade instead.

YOUR OVERALL STOPPING DISTANCE
Imagine you are driving along a quiet road at 30 mph, in good conditions, and all of a sudden, someone pulls out in front of you. By the time your brain acknowledges this information and you react by braking to a stop, you would have travelled a distance of approximately 23 metres (75 feet). On a wet, slippery road it is double that distance.

SEAT BELTS
Wearing a seat belt is not just a legal requirement – it makes good sense. Research shows that a person not wearing a seat belt can be seriously injured or killed in a crash when a vehicle is

travelling at speeds as low as 12 mph. If a baby is travelling in the car with you, make sure you use an approved baby carrier suitable for the child's weight. Failing to wear a seat belt may also affect your claim for compensation if you are involved in an accident.

TYRE BLOWOUT

If one of your tyres blows out, the car may pull to one side. The risk is increased if the brakes are applied. You should grip the steering wheel firmly, take your foot off the accelerator and roll the car to a stop by the side of the road at a safe and convenient place. Remember, if you use hard braking, this will only make things worse. Before you attempt to change the wheel, always move your vehicle to a safe and convenient place first. This is a sensible precaution to take as you may expose yourself to danger from other vehicles. Always carry a legal spare tyre and proper equipment to change a tyre in your vehicle at all times.

LOOSE WHEELS

If 'clanking' noises are heard, this may be due to loose wheel nuts. Slow down gently, stop and retighten the nuts. As a precaution, drive to a convenient garage where a mechanic can check the wheel, its nuts and bolts and wheel bearings.

If the wheel comes off, the car will drop at the affected corner, resulting in a strong pull to one side. Counter this by firm steering and gentle, progressive braking to bring the car to a halt. One important point; refrain from overtightening the wheel nuts as they may become impossible to loosen in an emergency.

SHATTERED WINDSCREEN

If your windscreen shatters when you are driving, you should punch a hole in the windscreen wide enough for you to see through. This will enable you to carry on driving until you decide it is safe to stop. If loose chippings are being thrown up at your windscreen from the road surface or from a passing lorry, the best protection to stop your windscreen from shattering is to place the fingertips of one of your hands hard against the glass. This absorbs the impact.

LIGHTS FAILING

If both headlights suddenly cut out, slow down quickly. Use any other source of illumination you have, e.g. fog lamps, spot lamps or emergency four-way flashers. They can all help you to drive at a slow speed to safety.

WINDSCREEN WIPERS FAILING
If your windscreen wipers suddenly stop during heavy rain, keep driving straight ahead. Crouch over the wheel and place your face close to the windscreen so that you can see where you are going and pull into the side of the road as soon as possible.

BRAKES FAILING
Should your brakes suddenly fail, pump the brake pedal on and off and apply the handbrake quickly but progressively. Do not yank it. Start selecting lower gears to act as a brake on the engine. Run the edges of your wheels against the kerb. If you have time, switch on your lights to warn other road users of your presence.

ENGINE FAILING
If the engine seizes up, this may be due to overheating caused by a broken fan belt or lack of coolant. Complete seizure results in the driving wheels locking. De-clutch immediately and move the gear stick into neutral. Check the mirrors, signal and move to the side of the road, making sure not to cut in front of other vehicles.

ACCELERATOR STICKING DOWN
In many cases, this is due to a broken throttle return spring. Do not try to lift the pedal with your foot. Simply check the mirrors, change into neutral, switch off the ignition (but do not remove the ignition key as this will cause the steering wheel to lock), coast to the side of the road without crossing in front of any other vehicles, and stop.

TRAPPED INSECT
If you are driving and you notice an insect such as a bee, wasp or hornet trapped inside your vehicle, do not lash out with your hand. This will only antagonise the insect and attract it to you. Open a window so that it can fly out. However, if this fails, pull into the side of the road and open the door also.

BONNET FLYING UP

Do not panic. Steer on the same course, braking progressively, signal and move carefully to the side of the road, again ensuring not to cut across any other vehicles. Winding down the driver's side window may assist forward vision.

COLLISION COURSE

If another driver falls asleep or loses control and his vehicle is heading straight towards you, you should sound your horn and flash your lights. Avoid driving onto the other side of the road, even if you think it is clear. The oncoming driver may wake up or gain control and pull left at the last moment. If you have to run off the road to avoid a collision, earth banks and ditches are far safer to hit than poles or trees. If it is impossible to run off the road, turn your vehicle at an angle to avoid a head-on collision.

AIRBAGS

Airbags are designed to protect you and your passengers in the event of a collision. They are becoming increasingly popular in certain models of cars. Airbags are most commonly installed on the driver's side only. The airbag is fitted in the centre of the steering wheel and it is designed to operate in the event of a significant frontal or front corner impact (about 18 mph), where the driver's head would otherwise hit the steering wheel, with the risk of serious injury. In the event of a serious crash the airbag will fully inflate in less than a second and it will make contact to protect the driver, then deflate to absorb the impact, again in less than a second after it has been activated.

FLOODED STREETS

On the approach to flooded areas, always drive through water at a very slow speed in a low gear. It would be prudent to leave your car and check the depth of the water and also for any hidden obstruction or subsidence. If the water is deep, slip the clutch and apply the accelerator to keep the engine running fast. Check your brakes afterwards to ensure the brake linings are dry.

DRIVING INTO DEEP WATER

Should your car happen to crash into deep water and become

totally submerged, it is highly important to remain calm during this emergency. You should allow your car to fill with water until the level is almost at the top. You should then take one last gulp of air before opening the door or window and swimming to safety. You will be unable to open the door prior to this because of the pressure difference, and if you open the window too early, too much water would gush in at once.

STRANDED IN SNOW

Weather conditions can alter rapidly during winter months. If your car gets bogged down in heavy snow and you cannot break free, it is crucial that you know how to survive until help reaches you. It is best to prepare for the worst as you may have to wait for some time. The will to survive varies considerably in human beings, but evidence shows that some individuals have been able to survive extreme winter conditions for very long periods of time. The most fatal mistake is to leave your engine running continuously, as you may fall asleep and then, because of the sudden cold die without recovering consciousness if the engine cuts out or runs out of fuel. It is safer to switch the engine off and on periodically in order to conserve petrol. To survive severe winter conditions you should keep the following points in mind:

- Have and maintain a positive mental attitude.
- Push negative thoughts out of your mind.
- Conserve energy.
- Exercise to prevent painful stiffness and to maintain body warmth. This must be carried out slowly and frequently to conserve energy and should not be overdone.
- Protect the body from cold and damp.
- Guard against boredom and depression. Keep yourself and any passengers occupied.
- Unless you know for a fact that help is near at hand, do not wander off in search of food. You may get frostbite or hypothermia.
- Ration any food that may be carried in the car.
- Light a fire as soon as possible. Ideally, light three fires in a triangle shape (this is an international distress signal). Consider using your car's cigarette lighter if you have no matches.
- Write the word "HELP" on the snow in very large letters so it

can be easily seen from the air.
- Cover your vehicle and the aerial with brightly coloured items so that you can be seen from the air by any rescue team. Remember to brush off any snow covering frequently.
- Never eat snow or ice as it will reduce body temperature and cause sore lips, gums and tongue. Always use melted snow or ice.

Remember, in cold areas exposure causes death before lack of fluids or food. Many deaths in the middle-aged and elderly are caused by strokes and heart attacks brought on by exposure to the cold. Research shows that within half an hour of considerable cooling of the body, blood becomes more liable to clot. Anyone suffering from exposure should be provided with heat as soon as possible.

Before setting off on your journey during severe weather conditions always ask yourself is your journey absolutely essential?

You should carry the following equipment in your car if you believe there is any possibility of blizzard conditions:
- Emergency food and water.
- Spare fuel.
- Shovel.
- Snow chains.
- First aid kit to include water purification tablets and lip balm.
- Knife and torch.
- Sleeping bag(s) or blanket(s).
- Metal container for heating food and water.

MOVING OFF IN DEEP SNOW

If you are starting off in deep snow and you encounter wheel spin, do not race the engine because your wheels will dig in further. To get round this problem you should move your car slightly backwards and then forwards until you break free. Use the highest gear possible. In these conditions, it is a good idea to carry a spade and place old sacks or car mats under your wheels so that your tyres can grip more easily, to stop your car being embedded in the snow. Always remove any heavy snow lying on top of your vehicle before moving off. When you brake, weight is transferred to the front of your car; any snow that has not been cleared from your vehicle's roof may suddenly fall onto the windscreen and your vision will be severely restricted. Many serious accidents have occurred this way.

Chapter 6

Evasive manoeuvring techniques

If you are attacked, there are several evasive manoeuvres which may be utilised and this chapter deals with each of them in detail.

THE J-TURN

If you find yourself in a situation where the road ahead of you is effectively blocked by another vehicle or obstruction and you cannot mount the kerb to drive round the hazard because of road-side furniture, you could carry out the J-turn. The J-turn will only succeed if the exit to your rear is not blocked. We shall now examine how to handle the car during this exercise. Imagine your car is in fourth gear and that you are travelling at 30 mph. (See Figure 18).

Making effective use of mirrors

Before you can make any safe driving decision, the first thing you must do is check your mirrors. The mirrors are the eyes in the back of your head and must be checked well in advance. Late use of the mirrors will lead to poorly organised and hurried driving decisions. A good driver will always know what is behind him and what is happening around the sides of his car.

Speed

If it is safe and the exit to your rear is not blocked, the next thing you should do is stop the car quickly and under control. To achieve this, you should be pushing the brake pedal harder as the vehicle slows down and try to stop well before the hazard if you can. Keep both hands on the steering wheel (because you will need as much control as possible) at the "ten to two" or "quarter to three" position (avoid wrapping your thumbs round the rim).

Escape route

As soon as you come to a halt, you must again look in the rear-view mirror. Avoid staring at it, you only need to take a quick glance in case the situation behind you has changed. If it is safe, you should now take hold of the gear lever firmly and select reverse gear, positively and distinctly, without looking down at the gear lever. After selecting reverse gear, you should return your hand back to the steering wheel and reverse quickly under full control. If you cause your wheels to spin, you will lose valuable time and you may be captured by your attackers, or worse! You must coordinate the use of the foot and hand controls so that you move the car smoothly and accurately.

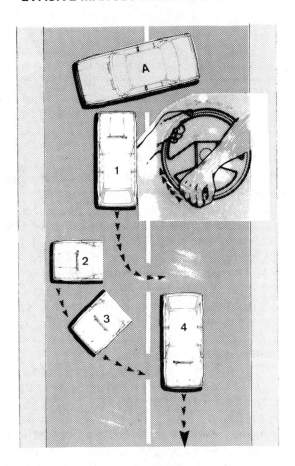

Figure 18. The J-turn.

Palm-down, thumb-down position

When you are reversing rapidly under full control, imagine the steering wheel as a clock face. Place your right hand in a position on the steering wheel, at seven o'clock. This technique is known as the "palm-down, thumb-down" position. When the car has built up sufficient momentum, take your foot off the accelerator and turn the steering wheel to the right as quickly as possible. Imagine throwing the steering wheel out the window. The weight of the engine will drag the front of the car round (anti-clockwise), and you will end up facing the opposite way.

Position

When the car is almost in its new position, take hold of the gear lever firmly, and quickly select first gear whilst tensing your right hand to give you more control of your steering. After you have selected first gear, you should return your hand back to the steering wheel and, using the foot controls smoothly, keep full control of the car when accelerating away.

THE TWO-POINT TURN

You may already be familiar with the three-point turn. The two-point turn basically achieves the same result but does not take so long to carry out. Imagine you are driving along and the road ahead of you is effectively blocked and it is impracticable to implement a J-turn because you cannot build up sufficient momentum in reverse gear. In this circumstance, you will find the two-point turn manoeuvre useful for turning within a limited space. The idea of the manoeuvre is to turn your car round to face the opposite direction using reverse then first gear. Since this manoeuvre has to be done quickly, you must be able to control your car and coordinate your clutch, accelerator and steering together. (See Figure 19).

The best way to remember how to do this manoeuvre is to split it into three stages. Remember the following code:
PREPARATION–OBSERVATION–MOVE

Stage 1: Preparation

Immediately you stop your car before the obstruction, you must select reverse gear. As soon as you have selected reverse gear, apply the accelerator and quickly let the clutch out until the engine note changes – feet still.

Stage 2: Observation

Quickly turn well round in your seat and look out the rear window because that is the direction in which the car will travel.

Stage 3: Move

Providing the road is clear, begin to move the car back quickly. Choose a place where you have plenty of room, where there are no obstructions in the road or on the pavement. Turn the steering wheel as far to the right as possible (full right lock) and aim to get your car at a right-angle across the road. As the car crosses the crown (middle) of the road, push the clutch down as fast as possible and brake, and stop the car before the kerb. You should

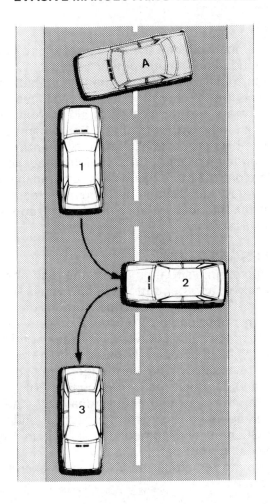

Figure 19. The two-point turn.

try to turn the steering wheel at least once to the left so that by the time your car stops, the wheels are straight ahead or possibly with a partial left lock on. Apply the handbrake quickly (if you are on an incline) and select first gear as fast as possible. Then move off to the left under full control without stalling or causing excessive wheel spin.

Remember the rule: "Keep the feet slow and move the hands fast".

TO SUM UP

You must remember to judge the camber of the road so that you will be able to judge how much power your car will need for the manoeuvre. In most roads, for drainage purposes, the highest point is in the centre (or crown). The crown slopes at either side down to the gutters and the degree of slope from the crown to the gutters is known as the camber. Some cambers are quite steep, other cambers are so small that, to all intents and purposes, you could be on level ground. It is obvious that the steeper the camber you are on, the more gas will be required in order to keep good control of your car. Remember, you must react immediately and carry out this manoeuvre very quickly or you will be at the mercy of your assailant.

THE BOOTLEGGER TURN

If you find yourself in a situation where the road ahead of you is effectively blocked, another option open to you is to execute the bootlegger turn. The term "bootlegger turn" is derived from the fact that often "bootlegging" whiskey dealers in Prohibition America had to make quick getaway. The idea of this manoeuvre is to turn your vehicle completely round within the width of the road without reversing. The bootlegger turn should only be attempted in a wide, quiet road. (See Figure 20).

Let's look at the way you should deal with the bootlegger turn. Again, imagine your car is in fourth gear and that you are travelling at 30 mph and someone pulls out in front of you, effectively blocking your path.

The best way to remember how to do this exercise is to split it into three stages.

Stage 1: Speed

As soon as you see the obstruction ahead, you should apply the footbrake straight away. Don't check the mirrors – there is no time (you should know what is behind you anyway if you are checking your mirrors properly). The footbrake should be pressed firmly and progressively, but under full control, to reduce speed to approximately 20 mph.

Stage 2: Gear

When you have your speed completely under control, you should change directly from fourth gear into second gear. Second gear should be selected in enough time to allow you to turn the car

Figure 20. The bootlegger turn.

around without striking the obstruction. The clutch at this point must be brought fully up which will assist you in braking and help to keep the car under control. I cannot stress enough that the clutch must be brought fully up throughout the manoeuvre – if you don't, you will not have maximum control of your car.

Stage 3: Escape Route

If you are driving on the left hand side of the road, turn the steering wheel briskly to the right and position the car right round in the width of the road (or vica versa). It is of paramount importance that you keep braking continuously throughout the

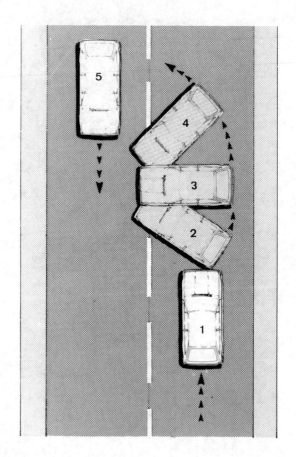

Figure 21.   The handbrake turn.

manoeuvre until the car is turned around in the direction you wish to go. As soon as you have positioned your car correctly, you should apply gentle pressure on the accelerator and take the correct safety line position in your new road. If you do not apply gentle pressure to the accelerator you may encounter a rear wheel skid.

Always remember the sequence, "brake before clutch". This manoeuvre can be hazardous because you may have to cross the path of oncoming traffic.

THE HANDBRAKE TURN

One other manoeuvre which can be undertaken is the handbrake turn. By pulling the handbrake up sharply and suddenly whilst the car is in motion and turning the steering wheel hard to the left or right, the car will immediately spin round in that direction. However, this is a very difficult manoeuvre to perform as control is almost completely lost and it is impossible to know what direction your car will be facing when it stops spinning, especially in wet conditions. (If you keep your foot on the accelerator the car will spin for longer.) Other manoeuvres described in this book are usually preferable in the vast majority of situations. (See Figure 21).

Chapter 7

Evasive ramming techniques

THE SINGLE VEHICLE RAM

You may find yourself in a life-threatening attack situation where the road ahead is effectively blocked by another vehicle. The road to your rear may also be blocked by another vehicle and so it is impossible for you to find an escape route to drive through. In this situation, you would have no alternative but to ram your way out. We shall now examine the single vehicle ram in more detail. (See Figure 22).

The correct procedure you should carry out to ram a vehicle can be remembered by using the following code:

- PREPARATION
- OBSERVATION
- MOVE

Preparation
If you are going to ram another vehicle, it must be done instantaneously. To carry out this manoeuvre successfully, the first thing you must do is try to stop your car about two car lengths from the obstruction. When you stop, your assailant will think that you have effectively given up, which is how an unskilled driver would normally react.

Observation
The most effective area of the target vehicle to strike is the rear (which has no engine weight), just behind the wheel arch. You should use the strongest point of your own vehicle, which is the front right or front left axle. This will absorb the shock into the target vehicle.

Move
You should now select first gear and accelerate as rapidly as possible, pushing your way through the vehicle. This will force the other vehicle around and it will strike anyone standing in the immediate vicinity. As you are coming through, and the other vehicle hooks on to you, don't worry, simply maintain acceleration and shake the steering wheel. This will cause the other car to vibrate loose. It is important to remember that you cannot just hit the target and expect to smack it out of the way: the idea is to push it out of the way. Always hold on to the gear lever and keep a firm grip on the steering wheel when you are ramming the other vehicle (but avoid wrapping your thumbs round the steering

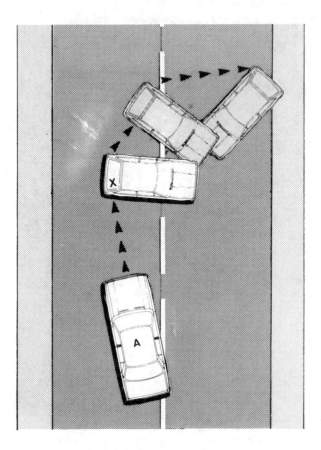

Figure 22. The single vehicle ram.

wheel rim). If you don't do this, the gear lever may jump out of gear or you may lose control of your steering.

To sum up

During impact, it is a normal reaction for drivers to come off the accelerator pedal because of noise and fear. However, it is crucial that you keep your foot hard down on the accelerator when ramming the other vehicle. If you don't, you will not have enough power to push your way through or your car may grind to a halt with your wheels spinning helplessly out of control.

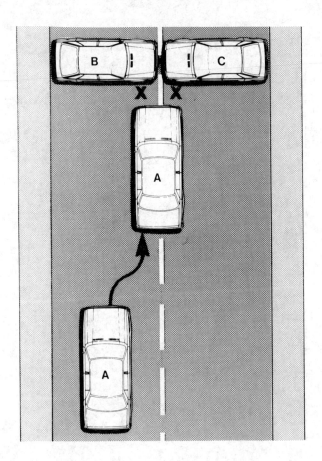

Figure 23.　The double vehicle ram.

DOUBLE VEHICLE RAM

Imagine you are driving along and you see ahead of you that two vehicles are completely blocking your path. The exit to your rear is also effectively blocked, preventing you from driving your way out. If this scenario occurs and it is impossible for you to drive round the obstructions, you will have no alternative but to carry out the double vehicle ram. This manoeuvre is similar to the single vehicle ram in that you are going to push the centre of your car directly between the two vehicles, at the point of least resistance. The idea is to push the two vehicles to the side and

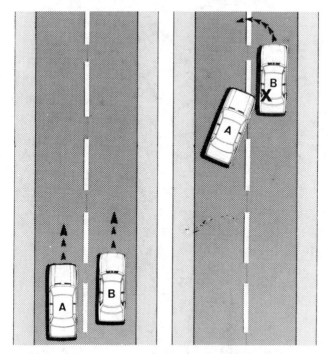

Figure 24. The moving ram.

open up a gap for your car to drive straight through. This will cause panic in the two drivers whilst anyone hiding behind the vehicles will be run over. (See Figure 23).

To accomplish this manoeuvre successfully, you should carry out the same procedure as for the single vehicle ram.

THE MOVING RAM

Imagine you are driving along the road and you find yourself in a situation where another driver has positioned his vehicle alongside your car, threatening you with physical violence and attempting to ram you off the road. In this circumstance, you have no alternative but to forcibly move him out of your way. This can be an easy manoeuvre to perform if executed correctly with proper timing. (See Figure 24).

Scan the road

When your car is in motion, keep an eye on what the other driver is doing and be aware of the general road and traffic conditions

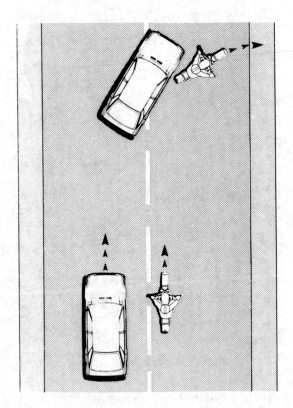

Figure 25. The motorcycle attack.

(make full use of peripheral vision). To move the other vehicle out of the way, you should adopt the following procedure.

Be patient

You must be patient and wait until the other driver starts to pass you. You can force him into this position by coming off your accelerator or braking suddenly. When he passes you, wait until you see his rear left-hand wheel in line with your front right-hand wheel.

Bumper to bumper

When this happens, you should steer briskly to the right and nudge your front bumper into his rear bumper which is the area just behind his rear wheel. As soon as you bump into his vehicle, immediately take your foot off the accelerator, as his vehicle will spin round in front of you helplessly out of control. The greater the speed at which your car is travelling when you hit the other vehicle, the faster the other car will spin out of control.

Remember

If you miss the point of contact and hit the other vehicle's door by mistake, this could be highly dangerous as the other vehicle will spin round directly in front of you and there is a strong possibility that you may hit the other vehicle side on. It is crucial that you hit the rear wheel arch of the other vehicle to avoid this situation occurring.

MOTORCYCLE ATTACK

Motorcycle attacks are becoming quite common, especially in Northern Ireland and abroad. Attackers favour the motorbike because they can quite legitimately be masked and gloved, and also because the rider can keep full control of his bike unhindered whilst the pillion passenger carries out the attack. It is also easier for a motorcyclist to escape as he has the freedom to ride almost anywhere once the attack has been carried out. To repel a motorcycle attack, it is crucial that you make proper use of your mirrors so that you can check the speed and position of any motorcycle attacking from behind.

You may then cut your vehicle into his path suddenly which will almost certainly terrify the motorcyclist causing him to fall from or overturn his bike. The angle of your car would also prevent the pillion passenger from aiming accurately. (See Figure 25).

Chapter 8

Car bombs

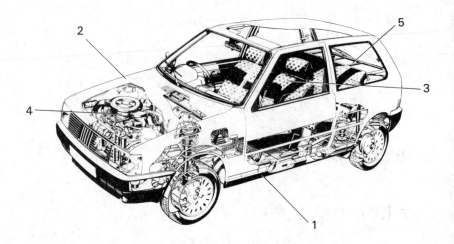

Figure 26. A systematic search is essential if you want to keep safe.

RECOGNISING THE RISK

This chapter is intended for anyone who feels they may be at risk from the threat of a car bomb. Car bombs are one of the most widely used terrorist weapons. They are generally aimed at members of the security forces, politicians or economic targets. However, a car bomb directed against economic targets usually incorporates a long-term strategy, designed to beat a government into submission for a political cause. In addition, the terrorist receives mass media coverage. Some capital cities have been targeted as specific areas for car bombs.

If a car bomb explodes, the effect can be devastating. It causes chaos and panic and it can even bring a city to a standstill. Warnings are sometimes given, but often there is insufficient time for the authorities to react. You can therefore help the security forces by being vigilant and by using the observation techniques in this book, even when walking along the street.

THE VICTIM'S MOTOR CAR

Many assaults, kidnappings and murders take place in or near the victim's motor car. On Monday 30th July 1990 the Member of Parliament for Eastbourne, Ian Gow, left his house shortly after breakfast and walked out to his Austin Montego car. When

Mr Gow drove out of the car port, his car was blown apart as the terrorists' bomb, planted directly underneath the driver's seat, exploded. The Member of Parliament, who was a personal friend of Mrs Thatcher, and her parliamentary private secretary for four years, was still alive when paramedics arrived at the scene; but he died as his shattered body was lifted into an ambulance.

VARIOUS TYPES OF CAR BOMBS
The type of terrorist explosive device will vary according to the nature and the expertise of the handler. There are two main types of car bomb that terrorists use; they are as follows:
(1)   A large quantity of explosives put into the boot of a car and hidden in a large container.
(2)   A small sophisticated device, usually placed underneath the victim's car when it is dark. When the victim drives the car, a trembler device detonates the explosive.

BOMB TRIGGERING METHODS
Self-acting devices – triggered by the victim
(1)   disturbing a trip wire,
(2)   applying pressure,
(3)   releasing pressure,
(4)   shedding light,
(5)   causing vibration.
Command detonated – set off by someone else
(1)   pulling a cord,
(2)   electric cable,
(3)   radio beam.

TIMERS
An electronic timer is normally attached to a bomb to make it explode. There are many different types of timers on the market. The most popular type used by terrorists is a memo parker timer (as used in parking meters). The more sophisticated electronic timers are based on the commercial timers found in video recorders. These allow the bomb to be primed months in advance. This technique was used by the IRA to try to kill the British Prime Minister, Margaret Thatcher, at the Grand Hotel in Brighton in 1984. Bombs attached to a timing device usually have a mercury tilt anti-handling booby trap.

VEHICLE SEARCH

A systematic search is essential if you want to keep alive. See
Figure 26). Search the vehicle in five areas:
(1)   Underneath.
(2)   Outside.
(3)   Interior.
(4)   Engine compartment.
(5)   Inside boot.
This section deals with the precautions you can take to guard
against a car bomb. Although there may be no known threat to
you at this present day and time, you must realise that a security
problem may well exist and common sense dictates that everyone
must consider the following general measures to reduce the risk
of an incident happening. Moreover, everyone must be alert,
vigilant and suspicious, as much for their neighbours and others
as for themselves.
- If you leave your vehicle unattended, always check your car
  for booby traps and devices when you return.
- Fit an anti-theft device to cover the whole vehicle.
- Close all windows and lock all doors.
- Park your car as close to a building entrance as possible.
- Park your car in a garage overnight.
- Always remove the ignition key when you leave your vehicle,
  even when it's in your own garage.
- Avoid leaving your vehicle unattended for long periods.
- Try and park where your vehicle can be seen.
- A thick bolt welded through the exhaust pipe will prevent a
  bomb being placed there.
- Flash cars draw attention. Use a low-profile vehicle.
- Do not use a walkie-talkie near the car until it is completely
  safe. It could detonate radio-controlled devices.
- If you see chunks of dirt on the ground, always be suspicious,
  as they may have been dislodged from under the car.
- If your car is garaged, sprinkle a fine layer of powder around
  the car at night and check that this has not been disturbed
  by the morning.
- Keep your car clean at all times. This will show up any dirty
  marks on the bodywork if someone has been tampering with
  your vehicle.
- When it is raining, someone may plant a bomb under your

car, hoping you will be lazy and drive off without first checking your vehicle. Make sure you do.
- Avoid routine.
- Ensure your movements by car are known to bona fide personnel.
- Park in a well-lit street.
- Check for bitter almond smell (explosives) or masking smell (perfume).
- If you are a well-known personality, never use obvious VIP parking spaces.
- Know your vehicle. This means remembering the layout under the bonnet well enough to spot any minor additions which could be a bomb.

REPORT THE UNUSUAL

Do not hesitate to advise the police of any suspicious person, vehicle or incident near the area where you park your car. Remember the registration number and description of a vehicle may be easier to obtain and more helpful than a personal description. Reporting anything unusual gives security specialists the chance to judge its significance.

DO NOT TOUCH

Should you become suspicious of any device at or near a motor vehicle, do not touch or tamper with it. Some of these devices are highly sophisticated and others very crude. Either way, they can explode, even with very gentle handling. Always remember that forensic scientists can tell from the way a bomb is put together who assembled the device.

ALSO FROM OTTER PUBLICATIONS.......

INCLUDES QUESTIONS AND ANSWERS TO HELP YOU PASS THE NEW LEARNER DRIVER EXAMINATION.

Now fully revised and into its third edition, the highly successful *Behind the Wheel* is aimed at both learners and their instructors – including driving instructors, friends and relatives. This step-by-step, easily understood, illustrated book provides instruction on how to drive correctly and safely on the road in twenty easy lessons. The teaching methods used are those laid down by the Department of Transport.

Behind the Wheel is unique as it covers driving instruction for the disabled, deaf and mute.

ISBN 1 899053 01 8   Price £7.95   270 pages

Please use your local bookshop to order your copy, or in case of difficulty, send a cheque for £7.95 (inc. p & p), made payable to Vine House Distribution, of Waldenbury, North Common, Chailey, East Sussex, BN8 4DR.